People Magnet

Transformative Habits to Attract Financial Success

(How to Be the Most Extraordinary Person in the Room)

Victor Burke

Published By **Gautam Kumar**

Victor Burke

All Rights Reserved

People Magnet: Transformative Habits to Attract Financial Success (How to Be the Most Extraordinary Person in the Room)

ISBN 978-1-7774070-4-9

No part of this guidebook shall be reproduced in any form without permission in writing from the publisher except in the case of brief quotations embodied in critical articles or reviews.

Legal & Disclaimer

The information contained in this book is not designed to replace or take the place of any form of medicine or professional medical advice. The information in this book has been provided for educational & entertainment purposes only.

The information contained in this book has been compiled from sources deemed reliable, and it is accurate to the best of the Author's knowledge; however, the Author cannot guarantee its accuracy and validity and cannot be held liable for any errors or omissions. Changes are periodically made to this book. You must consult your doctor or get professional medical advice before using any of the suggested remedies, techniques, or information in this book.

Upon using the information contained in this book, you agree to hold harmless the Author from and against any damages, costs, and expenses, including any legal fees potentially resulting from the application of any of the information provided by this guide. This disclaimer applies to any damages or injury caused by the use and application, whether directly or indirectly, of any advice or information presented, whether for breach of contract, tort, negligence, personal injury, criminal intent, or under any other cause of action.

You agree to accept all risks of using the information presented inside this book. You need to consult a professional medical practitioner in order to ensure you are both able and healthy enough to participate in this program.

Table Of Contents

Chapter 1: The Psychology behind Social Anxiety 1

Chapter 2: Identifying the Root 29

Chapter 3: Practicing Dbt 58

Chapter 4: Mastering the Art of Witty Banter 87

Chapter 5: A Guide to Charismatic Communication 102

Chapter 6: Improving Your People Skills 118

Chapter 7: Putting an End to Social Anxiety for Good 132

Chapter 8: Get Comfortable With Small Talk 154

Chapter 9: Create an Open and Approachable Vibe 166

Chapter 10: Find Common Ground 177

Chapter 1: The Psychology behind Social Anxiety

Growing up, I became outgoing and self-confident, till approximately the seventh grade, as quickly as I started out to experience shy and self-conscious. I don't forget the day that sincerely one in all my friends made amusing of me for making a shaggy dog story inside the the the front of a group of various kids, announcing it turned into "dumb". Looking lower back now, it might were a small difficulty, however I honestly felt embarrassed and humiliated. After that incident, I reconsidered the whole lot I stated in advance than speakme out loud. Although I continuously had a pretty appropriate humorousness, I turn out to be now feeling careful and I changed into maintaining decrease decrease back to avoid being made amusing of, even in informal conversations with my buddies. I actually have end up increasingly more quiet and lagged in conversations due to the fact I had to remember the whole lot I did and every word I stated.

By the time I turn out to be in excessive university, my identification felt like it became being lost and I didn't understand the way to genuinely be myself. I regularly had the equal thoughts looping thru my head about what I had stated or finished earlier in class or in social conditions. I modified into judging my very private behaviors, and feeling awful about myself, and I kept having the equal concerns approximately what ought to arise the following time I became out in public all over again.

I had social tension—the dread of performing some component that might make humans snicker at me or reject me. Social anxiety is the maximum commonplace type of tension teenagers face. While there are individuals who feel more snug as introverts their whole lives, there are loads of teens, like me, who want to be more social but sense awkward and socially tense, specially in center and excessive university, and even into university. But in advance than we take a look at how my past behaviors can also have a look at to your conduct, allow's begin with the basics.

WHAT IS SOCIAL ANXIETY?

When you feel shy, involved, or annoying, it is regular to experience the ones butterflies on your stomach, a racing coronary heart, and sweaty arms. But for hundreds of humans, this anxiety and strain experience overwhelming and make the ones situations even scarier. So frightening, in fact, that they revel in very uncomfortable taking element in everyday social conditions.

This is often called social anxiety or social phobia. These people don't need to experience like loners. They appreciate having buddies and generally experience being round human beings. But conditions like massive corporations or sudden social instances can purpose anxiety so extreme that they enjoy paralyzed. As a give up end result, they will not need to interact in sports activities or studies that they could otherwise revel in.

Everyone is special. Some human beings's emotions and reactions is probably an awful lot greater excessive than others. That's herbal, but no person wants to revel in honestly caught or unnoticed. Social tension is when someone's mind and feelings undermine their self-self assurance. Although it can experience similar to the end of the street, it doesn't need to be that way. There are easy topics that every person with social anxiety can do to help control their feelings, and experience higher!

Social anxiety ailment (SAD) is one of the most not unusual types of tension. Anxiety issues, in stylish, are the most commonplace form of intellectual fitness and nicely-being condition that people face. This can be felt at any age, but the starting of the condition is maximum commonplace around puberty and into younger maturity.

Teens who be afflicted with the aid of SAD typically don't have a massive network of buddies. They have a limited range of social contacts, display in particular terrible social talents, and can be troubled by college tension as nicely. In addition, having some other anxiety sickness, collectively with generalized tension sickness or separation tension illness, is also commonplace in young adults with SAD. The those who have a look at SAD factor out that the consequences related to the early onset of SAD encompass popular psychosocial and educational impairment, intellectual issues, depression, and in all likelihood in later years, substance abuse.

If it isn't addressed in advance than maturity, SAD can be associated with issues related to alcohol misuse, higher fees of divorce, an improved chance of suicide, and numerous types of psychopathology. Unfortunately, best a small percent of human beings get help for this undertaking, both as teens or possibly after they're adults. (Rapaport, 2016) The real statistics is, you've already taken a big step via way of choosing up this e book. You've got this!

WHY IS SOCIAL ANXIETY SO RAMPANT AMONG TEENS?

Social tension may be a problem at any age, however it's most usually seen in young adults. Some people with social tension contamination declare to have had it their whole lives; however, maximum humans turn out to be aware about that it first have become an hassle of their young adults. When we start to look at independence and start to define our role as teens, along with all of the duties that society expects people, young adults and teens have masses of obstacles to conquer, specially socially.

It is not clean to overcome those limitations, and the behavior patterns we shape as teenagers can also affect our lives in the future. Humans are social creatures by the usage of manner of nature. We all need to healthy in. Happiness and a experience of properly-being in relationships with one-of-a-kind people are key to our individual happiness and our enjoy of belonging in numerous businesses and internal our businesses. Some feelings of tension can be ordinary at some times, for some people. A "little" tension might be "ordinary" and feel like delight or hobby or an impetus for spurring us on and scary us in habitual or hard conditions. If you revel in involved whilst you make social mistakes, simply sufficient to observe from, that's genuinely quality.

But what if, like me, you discover yourself continuously traumatic about "messing up"?

What if you sense consisting of you're on diploma, within the spotlight, appearing for a totally judgemental target audience anywhere you move? What if you experience that each float you are making and each phrase you're announcing is being criticized? Social anxiety can notably impede your social lifestyles, teachers, and actually any and/or all of your pastimes, sports activities sports, and relationships.

It's vital to recognize that your anxiety is a mean combat-or-flight response. Your involved tool is responding to threats to your protection in exceptional the manner that it became intended to. However, the difference is that you aren't in real risk. Your concerned thoughts is continuously elevating the pink flag to guard you from an unsure condition.

Are you socially stressful, introverted, or simply shy? Social anxiety, shyness, and being introverted are form of comparable, however if you want to art work to your emotions, you should understand them extra exactly. Let's discover their variations.

Social tension motives a sense of shame and worry in human beings, and it is able to get within the manner of everyday functioning. Previously, it emerge as referred to as social phobia. People with social tension worry social situations due to the truth they receive as actual with they may be judged, embarrassed, or humiliated. They avoid social situations that they apprehend will cause them to disturbing or painfully undergo crippling struggling. That method they revel in anxiety out of proportion to the situation, which ultimately interferes with each day dwelling.

This experience is not like being shy. Shyness regularly consists of feeling reserved round human beings, but this surprisingly easy feeling of pain spherical unique human beings won't normally experience as genuinely debilitating because it does for individuals who revel in social anxiety.

Introverted human beings do no longer want or choice social interaction to enjoy authentically happy. That doesn't mean that they may be anti-social, but as an instance, they may go to a party, stay for an hour without interacting with quite some other humans and in fact leave once they sense geared up to do some issue one-of-a-type. They regularly revel in their time alone, now not because of the truth they worry interacting with someone, but due to the fact they don't want as masses social time. Conversely, extroverted people are exactly the alternative.

It's crucial to observe that each introverts and extroverts may be socially worrying and that it first-class turns into a problem once they have the selection to be with humans, spend time in a social state of affairs, and be in a public vicinity, but experience mainly annoying approximately what ought to rise up.

With social tension, you can experience moderate, slight, or excessive signs and symptoms and signs and symptoms. Some human beings awesome experience signs and signs at the equal time as in a particular setting. For example, I didn't like ingesting in public or maybe having to pick out out in which to sit down down down at lunch. For amazing people I knew, it changed into being called on through using a trainer in beauty, understanding wherein to hang around in the direction of recess, and so on.

People with minor social anxiety may additionally additionally interact in (or tolerate) social activities notwithstanding experiencing a few bodily and intellectual symptoms and symptoms of pain. These humans can participate in certain social sports at the same time as keeping off others. People with slight and fundamental signs can also moreover present with stronger reactions to precise social settings. I'm speakme approximately what's normally called a panic assault. As a end end result, folks that suffer from excessive social tension commonly steer clean of triggering social conditions the least bit fees.

Extreme social anxiety often manifests as signs and symptoms in severa procedures. When confronted with those conditions, anticipatory tension is fairly not unusual. Throughout your life, you can have skilled social anxiety at various tiers. No remember the extent of your feelings and testimonies, finding the assist that works for you is critical so you won't be held again with the beneficial aid of tension and you may be loose to do the matters that you need to do.

Now that you have some context. Let's return to my critiques and the psychology in the back of warding off human interactions and relationships.

"What if I say or perform a little factor stupid?"

This modified into my biggest worry. This dilemma made me calculate each movement because I desired to prevent looking silly. I occasionally even averted my friends because of the possibility that they may decide me negatively. I stayed silent in organisation chats once I felt at hazard. If I had a few factor crucial to mention, I might exercise it in my mind and reflect onconsideration on every body's possibly reactions. I each stated not anything or needed to calculate flawlessly the topics I had to say due to the fact I didn't want to be made fun of, or danger all of us disliking me.

Over time, this brought approximately large consequences. I joined in while youngsters had been making amusing of different people because of the reality, in the ones situations, the horrible interest wasn't on me. I changed into pronouncing and doing subjects that didn't experience like the actual me. Talking approximately different people in the lower back of their backs, and every now and then acting meanly immediately closer to them. This ultimately made me feel even greater out of place, so I'd flow lower again to my more reserved and quiet self. I grow to be afraid the opposite youngsters may additionally choose out on me if I wasn't greater talkative and on the middle of the institution. This intended I emerge as caught in an infinite circle of going from being withdrawn to bullying; to being class clown; to—honestly no longer me—all the at the identical time as retaining off the deeper trouble.

The extra I suppressed my herbal inclination to surely be myself in social times, the greater my involved thoughts sounded alarms approximately the perils of doing a little issue silly. I felt helpless in overcoming my inhibitions about becoming a member of really spontaneous conversations. I felt increasingly more remoted because of the fact the circle of humans I depended on narrowed. The greater I prevented social conditions or acted like a bully, the more I felt undesirable, making me avoid in addition social conditions like a vicious cycle.

Social anxiety ailment is one of the primary reasons of losing out of university and teen substance abuse. Social anxiety is likewise not unusual amongst college college students who are truly starting in a latest college environment, like center college or excessive faculty. SAD regularly will increase its unsightly head for college kids transitioning to college. When that factor of 12 months rolls round and university college college students gather popularity letters from instructional institutions, it marks the start of a latest financial ruin in their lives. For young adults suffering from a social anxiety disease, what need to be proud moments of newly confirmed self-accomplishment and independence can be met with blended feelings of happiness and determined worry. Spoiler alert! In case you haven't located, social anxiety typically worsens at the same time as it isn't treated.

I've heard people say things like, "They are truely shy. Once they start university, the entirety will alternate as they make bigger up." Unfortunately, that false impression can also moreover additionally surely upload pressure and cause students to reach out for terrible coping mechanisms. They can also begin believing that they will have the ability to overcome social anxiety with the aid of way of manner of getting under the influence of alcohol or stoned or discover one in every of a type unfavorable procedures to try to make themselves enjoy higher and relationships enjoy less complex.

As a result, many university students drop out of university, even supposing they're still of their first twelve months. What a backward, wasteful mistake and loss for teenagers who are decided to healthy in; they need to speak; they want to be a part of the company, and they need connections. Why are their brains constantly telling them they do no longer belong? What precisely is taking location in the brains of humans with social tension? And now for the era (thank you, Dad!)

THE NEUROSCIENCE OF SOCIAL ANXIETY

According to mind scans, the amygdala region of the mind is hyperactive in sufferers with a social tension sickness (McMurray, 2022). The combat-or-flight reaction, which prepares the body to react to perceived dangers (real or imagined), is introduced on thru stimulations within the amygdala. Rapid heartbeat, sweaty palms, breathing pride, muscle tightening, an boom in blood sugar stages, and a freezing of the thoughts that forestalls people residing with anxiety from thinking or reasoning usually are just a few of the signs and symptoms related to immoderate anxiety with the aid of the amygdala pastime.

The prefrontal cortex vicinity of the mind becomes the focus of hobby at the same time as people revel in a spike in anxiety. When no proper chance is present, the prefrontal cortex sends indicators to the amygdala that defuse its involved reaction. It's the prefrontal cortex's activity to calm those reactions via the use of evaluating them calmly and rationally. However, in folks that experience social anxiety, the prefrontal cortex amplifies in preference to reduces amygdala hobby. (Ho, n.D.)

No amount of logical contemplation can ease the problems that people with social tension revel in, for the reason that their brains understand social interactions as real threats because of their deeply ingrained fear about how distinct human beings will react. Fortunately, brains can be rewired to create new circuits and connections.

The anterior cingulate cortex (ACC) performs an vital characteristic in controlling feelings. It performs a big feature in coping with social pressure and soaking up social rejection. When someone is socially demanding, their ACC is overactive, and the ACC lets in amygdala-prefrontal cortex communique. This route is blocked for human beings who've social anxiety (Ho, n.D.). They locate it more difficult to control their feelings. This is why socially hectic humans often overestimate the poor consequences of hard social conditions and supply the possibility of social rejection this form of pinnacle priority.

Processing facial expressions and figuring out others' emotional states includes an area of the mind known as the fusiform gyrus. This is crucial facts for extremely good social interactions. Depending on the coping mechanisms the character has set up, the fusiform gyrus (a shape that spans the occipital and temporal lobes' basal surfaces) in human beings with social tension disorder can either be overactive or underactive. The fusiform gyrus can be much less lively if someone with social tension has made it a exercise to avoid making eye contact with different people. But the fusiform gyrus can be considerably extra energetic than traditional if the person focuses considerably on facial expressions.

This may also additionally provide an explanation for why socially demanding people occasionally misinterpret facial expressions or in any other case emotionally impartial facial reactions.

A funny instance of this for me as a youngster changed into the day I concept my dad end up mad at me. I turn out to be tip-toeing round conversations with him due to the reality I couldn't recognize why he modified into reputedly upset... until I observed out that he wasn't mad the least bit. He just had a toothache. If it changed into that clean to misread my very personal dad's reactions, even within the safety and security of my very very own residence, actually recall all the topics I in all likelihood misinterpret in one-of-a-kind regions of my existence.

The hippocampus plays a large feature in memory and mastering and additionally may be important in social anxiety. According to three records, social tension can be a behavior pattern human beings select out out up after numerous unfavourable social encounters (Swee et al. 2021). They extend familiar with specific behaviors over the years and count on terrible responses from notable human beings.

The hippocampus works additional time in socially demanding humans when they view the faces of new people. They in no way learn how to come to be aware of interacting with unexpected faces as with out problems as in the manner someone without that fear does. Instead, they keep classifying those faces as unstable. This explains why socially irritating people discover it considerably more difficult to fulfill new people.

To assist you apprehend, if you have social anxiety, the amygdala, a part of your mind that strategies fear, is more energetic while searching at sudden faces. This manner your mind sees the ones faces as more dangerous. Fear receives activated for your frame, making you sweat, making your coronary coronary coronary heart race, making you tremble, and making it difficult to respire. Remember, you are humanly stressed to look threats inside the environment. So while you meet someone new with a independent facial talents, that is most humans, you understand them as a hazard, and also you bear in mind they may be wondering harsh thoughts approximately you.

Because of these sensations on your body and loads of these mind floating round your head, now your hobby is most effective that specialize in those dangers. It will become hard to speak, difficult to engage, and difficult to keep a communique—all of the ones subjects rob you of getting real-global data approximately what human beings genuinely keep in mind you.

Many individuals who make bigger anxiety problems are more liable to experiencing tension, precisely because of the "Behavioral Inhibition to the Unknown." This method you may be inclined to go into reverse when in a brand new scenario. You might also understand what this looks like at the same time as you watch kids in their first few years. Have you found children try to disguise behind their parents to keep away from new and uncomfortable conditions? As we develop, we check new subjects and benefit new reviews. It's the surrender stop end result of those commands that create the inspiration of our mind and issues.

When we're uncovered to demanding or terrible conditions early in our lives, which incorporates fighting, abusive language, or feeling bullied in college, we partner similar activities with chance. And now, every time we are available in touch with folks which are similar to folks that brought on the ugly enjoy, our thoughts makes increasingly more establishments with people representing chance. Although you apprehend the ones humans are not probably to reason you any chance, you continue to can not overcome the sensation built on evaluations.

From my mind-set as a youngster, it's not unusual accountable your self for awkward situations and keep searching at topics that make you enjoy awesome. And while your mind starts offevolved offevolved along side all this stuff up, you consider you studied how regular and one-of-a-kind you are.

Basically, I go through in mind simply generally feeling terrible about myself.

When you've got social anxiety, it's virtually difficult to appearance the huge photo. Attention becomes slender and distorted. It's easy to get to a degree in which you are bringing your self down. Essentially, psychologically abusing your self. I'm speaking about the tendency (and I did this too) to location yourself down within the the front of others. To say terrible subjects about your self. And to even skip to this point as to harm your self physical. In hindsight, once I did those objects, I was hoping it would carry a few hobby to my conflict. It end up additionally a manner of in search of to sense on top of things, but glaringly, the ones weren't the maximum green coping mechanisms.

CONSEQUENCES OF SOCIAL ANXIETY DISORDER

People with social anxiety or social phobia typically experience excessive fear each time they're the middle of hobby. When this sense is related to specific physical symptoms and signs and symptoms, it's miles termed social anxiety disorder. This kind of excessive anxiety is generally observed with the resource of attempts to keep away from or break out from the events that reason it. People who be anxious through social tension frequently withdraw from the social context, each thru taking a much less lively feature inside the interactions which may be taking area or by using surely quitting the social hobby absolutely. Because humans revel in anxiety due to a wide range of factors, it's vital to distinguish among social tension and anxiety stemming from nonsocial belongings.

Not all instances of anxiety that get up even as in touch with particular human beings or which might be caused through other people are manifestations of social anxiety.

For example, in case you are involved due to the fact a person is abusive within the direction of you or due to the truth someone places you in a state of affairs in which you feel bodily or emotionally dangerous, then a 3rd party to your life is the deliver of your anxiety, now not you. It's important to understand this form of "regular/suitable" tension as a pleasant alert system for preserving you solid!

Looking at and being conscious of the differences amongst appropriate tension and social tension ailment can also additionally revel in complicated inside the starting, however it's critical to growing excellent thoughts pathways in existence. Consider the variations amongst a person doing or saying a few issue hurtful to you vs. Your very personal feelings at the same time as you are managing instead uncomfortable conditions; like starting or retaining conversations, introducing yourself to a person new, asking a person on a date, reaching out to a instructor approximately a query, attending sports, dances, or different social activities, ingesting in organizations, performing within the the front of others, sharing a ebook you wrote (I mainly enjoy the irony proper right here as a teen with social tension writing the e-book you're reading now), and so on.

People with social tension disorder can retrain their brains to react extra logically and thoughtfully in the route of social situations! No disclaimers, no horrible cautionary clauses! These cognitive-behavioral remedy techniques are end result oriented with capacity aspect outcomes, in conjunction with better shallowness, happier relationships with buddies and circle of relatives, alternatively a success sports and accomplishments in all elements of existence, and so on!

Chapter 2: Identifying the Root

Imagine that nowadays is the number one day of your new issue-time technique. You may additionally additionally feel traumatic or worried. You want to depart a super effect, do no longer you? This feeling is everyday. It's natural to have those feelings, and it's miles possible that having them will help make you more vigilant and watchful. On the opportunity hand, tension is typically decreased intensive when you've had a chunk of time on the challenge, and you get used to the obligations and characteristic had a hazard to get to apprehend your coworkers.

For a few people, the initial tension is powerful, maintaining that stage a good deal longer than they want to enjoy that way. The dread those humans revel in of being judged with the useful resource of recent people is so big that it interferes with their functionality to perform their duties successfully and do their manner. The fact that they may need to move somewhere in which specific people might be looking them should cause them to determine they didn't want to take the method within the first vicinity. This displays sincerely one of the disturbing situations of dwelling with social tension disease.

Remember, people who have anxiety troubles are all special. And despite the fact that maximum humans proportion masses of commonplace traits and reports, there can be a huge range of variations amongst each folks in phrases of the significance and kinds of situations feared. What works for me, or for a person else, may be one-of-a-type for you. But, so long as you are human (properly, in reality I'm experimenting with those thoughts on my cats too), the techniques in this e book are beneficial, in case you deliver them a hazard.

HOW SOCIAL ANXIETY DISORDER TAKES OVER

If this detail sounds a chunk greater dull, it's due to the fact my dad (Jonathan) is butting in with the research stuff. SAD sufferers can be prominent from those who do now not have the situation based on severa situations that they find out scary. The generalized SAD subgroup is characterised thru the use of fear in maximum social occasions and therefore money owed for around 1/2 of the sufferers who're searching for for treatment for anxiety. The non-generalized subtype is likewise characterised by a fear of specific social interactions however has normal functioning in others. According to the British Psychological Society and The Royal College of Psychiatrists (2013), the unique subtypes are excellent afraid of a few effective situations, for example, turning in a speech in a public placing.

We can reflect onconsideration on social anxiety disease as living alongside a continuum, with the appropriate subtype at one stop of the continuum and the non-generalized and generalized subtypes located in addition along the continuum due to the fact the type of feared situations and the diploma of purposeful impairment increase. The generalized subtype seems to be incredible from the opposite subtypes in that it normally manifests at a greater younger age than the opportunity .

The form of situation a person with SAD fears the most, together with being determined, performing, or interacting with others, is some other criterion used by clinicians at the same time as developing a diagnosis. In those situations, the mind reacts with fear or anxiety because of the fact the ones emotions clearly encourage us to avoid threats. Even even though this reaction has right intentions, mainly protecting the character from dropping social repute and being rejected, it usually does more damage than top due to the reality we can't constantly keep away from social and universal universal performance conditions, and being socially annoying whilst we must face them usually places our social wellknown performance at threat.

As a effect, stressful social sports activities have a large impact on the improvement of social tension sickness. This does now not most effective account for the activities we have had in our non-public lives. In truth, our brains likely get conditioned in reality by means of the usage of being uncovered to the painful social research of various humans, too. That is due to the fact someone's thoughts witnessing a person else having a awful revel in in the social realm; may probably interpret and are to be had to conclusions alongside these traces, "Hey, this kind of social situation is risky. Look how they laughed approximately that state of affairs and rejected them whilst he said it. You've were given to be alert, so this does not show as much as you."

This method that a person might also moreover learn how to be socially traumatic and frightened in social conditions due to the truth their thoughts noticed each person else having an awful revel in. Have you ever seen someone else being made fun of and worried that you can be next? How extended do you need to take a look at any shape of social media before you notice terrible comments? This form of conditioning is referred to as Observational Learning, and studies has examined that it is able to play a part within the development of social tension illness. (Selbing 2019)

IDENTIFYING THE ROOT CAUSE OF SOCIAL ANXIETY

Genetics, mind chemistry, demanding lifestyles sports, and trauma are idea to be among the organic and environmental reasons of hysteria troubles like SAD. Conversely, anxiety triggers are mother and father, locations, or matters that elicit an demanding reaction. It's doubtful precisely what motives social anxiety disorder, however an inherited predisposition to increase it is due to genetics. Look once more thru your family; if absolutely everyone else struggles with social tension, there can be an exceptional danger you may get the ones identical persona trends. (Sorry, Hailey—Ya, thanks masses, Dad.)

But more factors need to be present for the circumstance to arise itself. Individuals with a genetic predisposition may be extra vulnerable to particular environmental instances or mechanisms. The situation also can stop result from an interplay among person vulnerabilities, together with temperament, in addition to reactivity to strain, and environmental elements, which include reading reviews.

There are many capacity mental participants to the improvement of social anxiety disorder, e.G., direct conditioning, observational analyzing, statistics switch, and masses of others. Many research placed direct conditioning in patients identified with SAD. These times blanketed annoying sports that played a characteristic in the development of the sickness. The outcomes of early life trauma have been tested to have a desensitizing have an effect on on cortisol reactivity, mainly in the context of social tension sickness. Impairments cause avoidance behaviors in cortisol reactivity, important to persistent fear responses. These responses can also play an crucial element in the psychopathology of social tension. There is a hyperlink among disturbing studies in childhood and an stepped forward hazard of developing internalizing (which consist of most vital despair and social anxiety) or externalizing (which encompass delinquent personality disease and drug use) problems later in existence. (Young 2019)

In addition, there may be the possibility that various factors are predisposing and retaining elements. The development of social tension infection can be recommended with the aid of using many elements in the circle of relatives environment, which include the character of the dad and mom similarly to their parenting fashion and abilties (Hey Dad, you're listening to this, proper?). There are many strategies wherein dad and mom' activities could probable effect their children's psychopathology. A genetic tendency for anxiety may be surpassed down from parents to youngsters (Yes, I am. And, I apologize again, Hailey).

The dad and mom may additionally moreover limit the capability of the teenager to take part in social gatherings. Anxious people can skip it without delay to others via assertion, studying, and modeling. Particularly, parental shielding sports appear to perpetuate avoidance behaviors in demanding youngsters through reinforcing traumatic behaviors and discouraging seasoned-social behaviors. This is executed to defend the youngsters from potential horrific consequences. In addition, there may be a correlation among mother and father' inclinations within the direction of overprotection and their rejection of their children who display off signs and symptoms of social anxiety.

People who've professional bullying or distinct forms of humiliation, which includes rejection, own family conflict, sexual abuse, or different worrying events of their early years, are much more likely to get social anxiety illness. When they reach their overdue teen years, children who are very quiet or clingy can be at risk. An look or circumstance that attracts attention, which consist of facial disfigurement, stammering, or tremors due to Parkinson's disease, can growth feelings of self-awareness in a few human beings. It has been established that the generalized form of SAD has a bigger genetic element associated with it. And it is noteworthy that the opposite subtypes show large physiological reactions at the same time as they may be hooked up acting times like public speakme.

SITUATIONS THAT EXACERBATE SAD

The following bullets are some situations and situations that, extra frequently than no longer, make contributions to the development of social anxiety in young adults:

A adolescence spent with dad and mom or guardians who're overprotective, controlling, limiting, or nervous

Excessive social isolation, especially reading by myself in instructional conditions

Terrifying acts of bullying

Parental abuse. Abuse can take many paperwork, which encompass emotional, bodily, sexual, or verbal. Neglect is also a shape of abuse. Failing to renowned or validate a infant's concerns, diminishing them, or pretending they do not exist, is neglectful. Unfortunately, that is a high-quality cause teenagers boom SAD.

There are pretty some not unusual environmental motives for developing SAD. This list does now not cover they all but be looking for symptoms and symptoms associated with:

Addiction to pills or withdrawal from tablets

Excessive reliance on communique techniques that aren't direct or face-to-face (together with almost the entirety completed for your smartphone)

Conflicts inside the circle of relatives (especially divorce or violence)

People in your surroundings who are not accepting of you or who discriminate in competition to you because of additives of your identity (together with sexual orientation, values, or ideals)

Family records of highbrow contamination

RECOGNIZING YOUR ANXIETY TRIGGERS

Anxiety triggers are topics your thoughts has located to view as risky. As a result, the ones triggers result in acute anxiety symptoms and signs; like feeling stressful, upset belly, and shortness of breath. Not only are anxiety signs and symptoms unpleasant, but they also can result in lasting conduct adjustments. For instance, if you get heat and purple within the face, you are more likely to need to keep away from those sorts of social sports activities to prevent that sensation from taking area yet again. For people with SAD, maintaining off social occasions, teachers, sports activities activities, one-of-a-kind thrilling possibilities, or maybe common sports activities sports like going to the grocery save also can emerge as commonplace.

Fear of acting in front of people: Performing inside the the front of humans is one of the maximum common triggers. Sports competitions, diploma performances, and public speakme are all commonplace examples. People with SAD who're afraid of those situations often feel like their tension prevents them from doing some thing they could in any other case need to be doing. It can be tough for a teen to wait college or university and participate in extracurricular sports activities activities like specific teens. It may be hard to collaborate with people due to the fact absolutely the concept of running in a collection also can grow to be a purpose.

Difficulty in making and retaining conversations: A room whole of strangers is a few other big purpose for human beings with social tension illness. For me, it became specially a room whole of different young adults. If you have got SAD, meeting new human beings or attending a celebration wherein no person is aware about you is hard. For many humans, small talk makes for clean communique starters amongst strangers. However, for a person with social tension, making small speak isn't smooth. It can be even greater tough for humans who have SAD and are extra introverted.

You likely already apprehend that being suited at small speak will let you strike up discussions, form connections, and enhance your social skills. You might also additionally have additionally found out that keeping off small speak altogether will make your anxiety even worse. This is because of your worry of pronouncing the wrong detail or coming off as awkward even as making small speak. The difficult detail is which you are possibly going to feel like you'll want to practice the opening line time and again once more earlier than developing a flow into and your anxiety may additionally further increase if the stranger or friend you are trying to strike up a communication with is someone you are trying to affect, which incorporates an influential peer, teacher, or boss.

Ok, brace your self! Coming up, I'm going to challenge you to make a element of overcoming your worry of small talk. We will communicate greater about the manner to deal with tension within the coming chapters of this e-book, too.

Dating can be disturbing for each person. But for a person with SAD, it can be downright overwhelming. Let's be real; all people gets apprehensive once they meet a person new. But for teens with SAD, this courting anxiety is a super deal extra severe, lengthy-lasting, and placing aside. Virtually each difficulty of relationship can bring about improved anxiety signs and symptoms. While a few teens may additionally say that this is why they trust they're happier to be single or that their lives are already too whole to in form right right into a dating with every body else, the center reason they can't divulge heart's contents to a courting is because of their everyday awful mind regarding self-disgrace, embarrassment, and worry of rejection.

Anxiety while writing: This one may also experience super, however it's miles right. SAD sufferers may moreover experience tension while writing topics that they've to or want to percent with particular humans. This tension normally consequences from the concept that people will note something from your trembling arms as you type to the dread of studying your thoughts aloud in the the front of others. As with unique examples, writing anxiety generally comes from an unsightly experience within the past. It's smooth to become fearful of rejection, embarrassment, mockery, or criticism that may come with writing.

Perhaps you may have obtained criticism for some issue you wrote, your handwriting, or for expressing an emotion that feels embarrassing. Now, each time you want to put in writing in class, you have got got a panic assault remembering a past experience. This strongly conditioned response can also moreover produce and ingrain tough, horrible perception patterns to alter or conquer. Other problems, like a pervasive loss of shallowness or a worry of complaint, also can bring about a fear of writing phobia. Fear of writing may prevent end result from a fear of excessive success (yes, this is an actual element).

Sometimes it is simply that you are deeply scared of writing because it makes you revel in uncovered. Just as in other social anxiety conditions, you worry that all and sundry who reads it'll possibly be crucial and judgmental of you.

Phobia of eating in public: Your social life, school, venture opportunities, and most significantly, your physical health all go through when you have a phobia of consuming in public. Typically, eating and consuming are part of regular social interactions. Every day, there are a couple of sports activities on the same time as someone attends meetings, social gatherings, or one in every of a kind occasions that arise round mealtime. It can be confusing and overwhelming the way to behave in university cafeterias, fancy eating places, or at a person else's residence. If you enjoy immoderate anxiety whilst consuming and eating in front of humans, you would in all likelihood start declining invitations or adjusting conditions to most effective the ones that don't require eating within the front of other humans.

Company, environment, and state of affairs (or people, place, and element) can all function triggers for fear of ingesting and consuming in public. For maximum people with an ingesting phobia, the diploma of tension will growth based totally completely at the perfect logistics of the manner difficult the meals is to eat. Typically, finger meals provide the least hazard. Salads, soups, and meals with sauces are regularly the foods that make people revel in the maximum stressful. Spaghetti, as an example, has a higher threat of being messy even as ingesting, making it much more likely to create anxiety. Drinks often have little effect on anxiety, whilst those greater vulnerable to go away stains, like crimson wine, can also need to make human beings sense greater traumatic as nicely.

But why does this anxiety rise up within the first place? What is so hard about consuming in public? All of this anxiety stems from a deep-seated dread of receiving negative judgment from others. According to investigate from 2015, social tension and a few competencies of ingesting issues are related in detail because of this fear of receiving damaging remarks (Cuncic 2022). When someone is ingesting in public, many stuff can bypass incorrect; your fingers may want to possibly shake, your meals may additionally spill, you can appearance unattractive while eating, and you will probable get food stuck in your teeth or for your beard (Ha, ha, ha, Dad...) and so forth. Although generally, folks that don't have social tension do no longer pay masses interest to this, someone with SAD continuously issues that this type of activities can also take region to them, ensuing in embarrassment or rejection.

Fear of voicing your opinion: Do you hesitate to voice your opinion? Do you go with great human beings's reviews even whilst you disagree? People with social tension generally tend to forestall answering inquiries and are regularly reluctant to specific their mind because others will pick out them. The identical damaging or previously painful activities that purpose extraordinary social phobias normally motive opinion phobia.

Parents, teachers, or caregivers are regularly in fee for inflicting a teenager to expand this form of phobia. Constantly warning or criticizing a teen also can purpose them to revel in chronic suppression. A little one who has professional abuse or trauma is likewise much more likely to growth this phobia. Their self notion is averted, and their vanity plummets. The failure of people to express their perspectives have become defined perfectly via Noelle Neuman in his precept, "Spiral of Silence." He contends that humans continue to be silent due to the following:

People dread social isolation and are privy to the moves with the intention to make it more likely that they may revel in it

People are reluctant to voice their minority mind, in most instances out of problem approximately being rejected with the useful resource of others

People very own a "sixth experience," which permits them to determine the consensus without get right of entry to to surveys. (Simpson, 2014)

The functionality to voice your very own critiques is tough for everybody. But for human beings with SAD, this turns into overwhelming and complex due to the reality first of all, they face traumatic situations in making social contact and interacting with others and secondly, they risk going towards the social modern to set up their private opinion, this is some thing they already warfare with because of their loss of self-self guarantee.

Eye contact anxiety: As the decision indicates, an man or woman with eye contact anxiety may additionally avoid making eye touch at the equal time as talking to a person. If they do control to provoke eye contact, they will enjoy feelings of scrutiny or judgment. Anxiety over eye contact can hinder ordinary social relationships. Maintaining clean eye touch is generally visible as an crucial part of tremendous social engagement. People are seen as best and hospitable after they look someone else in the attention. However, this trouble of verbal exchange can be tough for lots socially nerve-racking human beings. People with SAD often revel in looking a person in the eyes as uneasy and anxiety-frightening. This kind of anxiety may additionally moreover have a genetic issue. According to investigate, human beings with SAD strongly dislike making eye touch.

If you've got SAD, eye touch may also additionally activate your amygdala (consider, this amygdala? It's the place of your thoughts that signs you to danger). Being on protect and avoiding emotional and social stimuli are each elements in social anxiety. As a end end result, one example can be that if you are at a celebration, you is probably alert to appearance out for folks who appear to be comparing you and also try to avoid instances in that you experience criticized. Therefore, it's now common for human beings with social tension to keep away from making eye contact in popular.

However, if you revel in pain whilst you're making eye touch however have no longer been recognized with an tension sickness, you may growth your tolerance thru difficult your self to make extra eye touch over the years or by using using opportunity practice strategies, which we are capable to talk approximately in more element later on this ebook too.

Fear of Being Socially Awkward: The fear of doing some aspect uncool often affects how people with social tension feel and, as a give up quit end result, how they have interaction with others. After engaging socially, the individual will pass returned of their thoughts and mirror on their conduct and probably choose out themselves with the aid of way of thinking that the whole lot they did end up bad. Many humans stricken by social tension disease will make a concerted try to keep away from social events and social touch. Still, in the event that they cannot do so, they may live out of the way and try and depart as brief as viable. This is clearly sad because of the reality whilst this takes area, they deprive themselves of the chance to have profitable reviews that could notably make a contribution to their extraordinary of life and efficiently combat their anxiety and self-deprecating, dangerous beliefs and sentiments.

Socially apprehensive people may additionally furthermore engage in what they speak with as steady conduct to reason them to feel more comfortable in social situations. Examples of this consist of mixing in or being silent, staying near acquainted faces, keeping off eye touch, or likely turning to substance abuse to enjoy tested or to accumulate their courage.

Although such actions can also moreover revel in like temporary answers, they'll be (no much less than) now not powerful long-time period social anxiety management strategies. Similar to avoidance, protection behaviors save you people consisting of you from demonstrating your inner social competence and actual self because you're continuously hiding in the lower lower back of a few issue or someone else.

Remember, your ultimate motive is a good way to discover ways to be confident in who you are, surely the way you're. That doesn't suggest you gained't make errors, say beside the point subjects, do loopy stuff, get poppy seeds caught on your teeth, or be embarrassed at times, however it does imply that you could brush or snort the ones off as you enjoy and create big relationships and situations at some point of your lifestyles.

Most human beings tormented by social anxiety infection have 3 or 4 situations that make them experience fantastically disturbing, and they'll do a little aspect in their power to keep away from those exposures if possible. Even mild quantities of anxiety signs and symptoms in social sports may be unsightly and may make your lifestyles sense more hard than it wants to be.

Ok, all that, so right proper right here's the good records! Ultimately, this is all internal your manage. It's no longer smooth, and it takes practice, but most of the time, plainly we are the precept occasion/character retaining us lower lower returned from overcoming our very non-public social anxiety disease. Our thoughts and feelings create the roadblocks that prevent us from progressing.

It's smooth to get sucked into the trap of social tension, of having terrible opinions approximately ourselves and denying our capability to deal with social occasions. Our self assurance can be decreased as a result, making it extra tough for us to make incredible modifications. But you're already developing a alternate via analyzing this ebook and showing a willingness to attempt! You have the opportunity to have interaction with others and become the confident, resilient, exciting, and tasty person you're and need to share with others.

Chapter 3: Practicing Dbt

Remember, social anxiety disorder is commonplace. It may also additionally experience overwhelming and prefer an no longer feasible lure to break out, but don't be fooled, due to the fact definitely, there are easy gear and powerful techniques that will let you navigate this labyrinth of emotions. We're going to tell you approximately DBT. It's a large extended call or three clean letters for a flexible and powerful method of training and helping to triumph over struggles of worrying thoughts and crippling tension. Ultimately, DBT will positioned you lower back on top of factors of your life!

WHAT IS DIALECTICAL BEHAVIOR THERAPY (DBT)?

DBT can be taken into consideration a modified form of cognitive-behavioral remedy aimed towards young adults to help them in greedy their emotional and inner conflicts efficaciously. Its primary desires are to teach people on the manner to be gift, create healthy coping mechanisms for stress, control their emotions, and decorate their interpersonal connections. ("The Center for Addiction and Mental Health", n.D.)

DBT allows benefit this with the aid of way of teaching human beings how to distinguish amongst what's real vs. What is a notion. We get hold of as genuine with that DBT is one of the best strategies for young adults to overcome social tension disease as it is easy and tangible, and consequences can come quick.

Although it modified into first of all designed for treating borderline persona illness, DBT has now been identified as a beneficial restoration intervention in treating a vast range of various conditions. This is especially interesting due to the fact, for hundreds people with social tension disorder, there can be specific worrying situations we want to find assist for as properly. DBT is assisting teens and teens who're struggling with any of the subsequent:

Depression,

Generalized tension sickness

Suicidal behaviors

Impulsive behaviors

Eating issues

Drug or alcohol abuse

And lots extra.

What makes DBT extra powerful than different conventional strategies of remedy is that it makes a speciality of supporting humans take shipping of and stability thoughts and emotions rather than select or emphasize one unique concept or emotion over some other.

HOW DOES DBT WORK FOR SOCIAL ANXIETY?

As said previously, using dialectical conduct remedy allows set up a balance between the blessings of trade and the validation (popularity) of who you're. (Cleveland Clinic, 2022) The first detail is to recognize and validate that your behaviors "make sense" in slight of your specific memories. Then, the second one difficulty is to discover whether the ones behaviors are, in reality, the nice movement for resolving an trouble. Using this proper judgment, you may choose out out new and critical capabilities to help you to manipulate your feelings and experience on top of things in social settings. DBT will assist unharness yourself assure and amplify the arrogance wished to triumph over social anxiety.

Our feelings have a big have an impact on on our lives. When danger to our existence, fitness, or properly-being lurks round, worry may moreover push us to behave and shield ourselves; therefore, number one feelings associated with tension, along with worry, can every now and then make wonderful enjoy. However, those emotions might possibly ground at the same time as there is no real threat of hazard, in which case they may be completely unproductive. These unproductive emotions can be difficult to address, primary to tension or maybe distress. DBT entails using your emotional and cognitive capabilities and making use of the ones device for your every day lifestyles. It gives a manner for addressing tough or maybe painful feelings and strengthens your capability for emotional law.

Core mindfulness: One of the easy abilities that DBT allows you construct is middle mindfulness. Mindfulness is the ability to live within the second and reputation on the here and now as opposed to dreading what's growing within the remote destiny. This assists you in growing a nonjudgmental consciousness of what's taking place inner of you (your thoughts, emotions, sensations, and impulses) and what's taking location outside of you (what you observe, listen, heady scent, and speak to).

People mistakenly partner mindfulness with education meditation, however in DBT, the idea includes a good deal extra than that. I name this the "attention muscle" and, as with every other muscle, training and strengthening it is essential. Having a strong "interest muscle" allows you to pay attention greater efficiently at the modern-day moment in location of residing on the past or destiny. This is specifically vital for those with tension problems who commonly tend to loop on subjects from the beyond or future.

Another mindfulness concept that I much like the utilization of myself and sharing with different teens is the concept of a realistic thoughts — performing from a place that balances each what is rational and emotional. For teens with SAD, this means acknowledging anxieties and being attentive to our emotional united states of america on the same time as concurrently tough ourselves to assume logically about the scenario as well. For example, if I'm skateboarding by myself, and all at once a collection of other teenagers suggests up on the park, my emotional self can also moreover lead me to need to do one element while my rational mind desires me to perform a little element else. But, as soon as I am conscious and the usage of my realistic mind, I can concentrate to both my emotional and logical voices, and as I do that, I commonly give you an awesome better opportunity that balances them every and enables me live in the game.

When you're experiencing tension, mindfulness talents will assist you slow down and deliver attention to powerful exceptional movements that you could create in any scenario. In addition, mindfulness competencies will help you maintain your composure and keep you from making impulsive selections which you can otherwise remorse.

Here is an exercise if you need to look at. Keep in thoughts that just like some other capability you're learning, the extra you workout this exercise, the faster and much less complicated it receives.

Whenever you revel in pressured, take a moment to examine your emotions and ask your self to understand how you are honestly feeling.

Next, ask your rational self what's genuinely taking region around you and to you.

Now, slowly and carefully, ask your thoughts to evaluate the differences maximum of the actual vs your perceived danger in this situation.

Finally, with all that beneficial statistics, stability your emotional and rational senses and voices and ask your smart thoughts the way you need to address this unique scenario at this particular time. (Be sure and stay with the prevailing and overlook about past or destiny fears!)

Distress tolerance: It's important to keep in mind that there are a few matters we control, a few topics we simplest have effect over, and hundreds of things which might be sincerely out of our manipulate. Distress tolerance permits you manage the distress you sense at the same time as things are from your direct manage with the useful resource of learning to simply accept your self simply as you're and the triumphing state of affairs absolutely the manner they are. To try this, there are four number one techniques that you could use any time you want them:

Self-soothing: Identifying a few element that feels comforting to you. This might be being attentive to track, taking a tub, journaling, or preserving an item that makes you enjoy better.

Distraction: This is often a quick-time period answer, but can be very useful whilst you need a 2d to regroup. This might be playing a recreation, looking a display, listening to music, workout, or doing a craft assignment.

Radical attractiveness: This is as radical as it sounds. It's genuinely accepting that some element is happening that you may't exchange, and mentally figuring out that the situation is surely the manner it is.

T.I.P.P.: This is my personal favorite. It's Temperature, Intense Exercise, Paced Breathing, and Paired Muscle Relaxation. For the temperature, I every so often want to splash cool water on my face. For exercising, even a few jumping jacks may be beneficial for me. Boxed breath (counting the period of my breaths gently) or any respiratory exercising is my glide-to method. And for paired muscle relaxation, I also locate that tensing my muscle corporations and exciting them (like tightening my legs and wiggling them unfastened) is also very useful. ("Peiper" n.D.)

Distress tolerance is in the end about recognizing that there are lots of factors occurring in our lives that we've got little or no or no manipulate over. Life itself can be overwhelming, but through using the ones strategies, you can learn how to see even the most difficult life conditions objectively and be capable of take shipping of these times with a assured experience of manipulate over your very own thoughts and feelings. For people who act too fast due to the fact they will be capable of't stand being dubious about situations, knowledge and incorporating distress tolerance may be in particular useful.

Interpersonal effectiveness: A essential motive of tension is the concern of being rejected, disregarded, and embarrassed via others. Interpersonal effectiveness let you experience extra fantastic approximately human relationships. Instead of that specialize within the entire factor that could skip incorrect, this device lets in you awareness on everything that may pass proper. This lets in cultivate thrilling connections, and empathy for others, and cultivates kindness and compassion in the direction of yourself similarly to others via DBT. It moreover teaches you to with a chunk of luck stand through your ideals and thoughtfully recommend in your values.

To workout interpersonal effectiveness, consider the acronym G.I.V.E.:

Gentle: Don't attempt to insult, assault, threaten, or pick out your self or others. This will make contributions to the negativity that might get worse your anxiety.

Interest: Even clearly pretending to be conscious of the out of doors global assist you to create hobby vs reactive fear and assist you focus heaps an awful lot much less on intrusive, traumatic thoughts on this unique scenario

Validate: Looking at topics from others' views can help you recognize, stability, and validate theirs and your private reactions to perceived threatening conditions.

Easy: Smile; smiling can be an effective and smooth manner to physically re-smooth your tackle matters or sure, to take manipulate, and consciously "trick" your thoughts into feeling snug.

Emotion law: You can also cope with excessive tension successfully with my desired device, emotional control. Emotional manage lets you be planned in advance than performing below tough times. It can help you preserve your composure, reduce your anxiety, address your fear and misery, and educate you to pay interest on sports activities that experience right to you, diverting your interest a ways out of your feelings of anxiety.

The primary purpose of growing your emotional regulation capabilities is to reduce your publicity to icky emotions with the beneficial useful resource of the use of techniques to govern any awful feelings that can rise up. Sleep, a balanced healthy eating plan, exercising, and wonderful healthful sports activities that make you experience appropriate can assist lessen your emotional vulnerability. None of those are especially easy for us teens, but they will assist hundreds!

You can also exercising some different essential DBT principle: performing in competition on your feelings at the same time as they may be unjustified via the situation accessible. Acting in opposition to worry and tension is a difficult but powerful way to reduce your tension. Confronting your fears in place of giving in to impulses to keep away from them will cause reduced tension and higher coping mechanisms. It takes courage to stand up for your very very own feelings, but you may be shocked with the useful resource of the way proper the final outcomes will revel in whilst you pick out to face and conquer your emotions.

Remember, your anxiety can show up from past awful feelings and thought styles. The bodily adjustments that you revel in because of anxiety are all derived from those lousy emotions. So even as you grasp emotional regulation, you'll feel physical stronger and in addition resilient to overcoming the ones undesirable feelings. Emotional law can provide you with your particular superpower as you beautify your capacity to apprehend and balance your thoughts, reactions, and anxieties added on with the aid of situations that previously felt from your manipulate.

The number one intention of DBT is to defuse terrible emotions that consist of social interactions. To get to this diploma, it is essential to recognize wherein the ones emotions come from and why they increase inner us. One of the essential factor factors of DBT that units it apart from one in all a kind healing strategies is "knowledge and acknowledging", which inspires the centered and nonjudgmental announcement and description of feelings and the manner they experience to you.

Understanding your feelings can appear to be noticing even as you revel in anxious and how you understand you are feeling demanding. Do you enjoy like throwing up? Crying? Or taking walks away? It can arise in all certainly one of a type strategies, and gaining knowledge of the way it feels to you is essential to running with and overcoming your anxieties. Acknowledging your fears seems like accepting your bodily and inner feelings as they are. It also can sound backward or incorrect, but feeling your anxiety can truly lower it.

When we take a look at our tension, we're able to understand ourselves better and that offers us the energy to make coping with tension masses easier. This is due to the reality through way of manner of operating closer to the capabilities, you allow your mind to differentiate among what is absolutely an emotion vs a fact so that you can successfully address bad feelings and perception styles.

WHY SHOULD I TRUST THIS FORM OF THERAPY?

I'm sharing this with you because it has worked for me, and I've seen it artwork for unique teenagers I recognize too. Over the years, I've worked with unique humans, therapists, drug treatments, and coping mechanisms (outstanding and terrible). I virtually have experimented with lots of techniques and techniques to manipulate my social tension disorder. I come to be hopeful and diligent time and time once more, however my very personal social tension endured to be a hurtful venture from center school to high school. Although I however have social anxiety, DBT has allowed me to have a greater feel of manage and strength.

With DBT, I understand I even have my very very own back. DBT gives me with assets and equipment I can use everywhere, on every occasion, in some unspecified time in the destiny of my life, to help myself accept and apprehend a way to balance my feelings with fact as I circulate via my anxiety into happiness for myself and others.

When I began walking with a therapist who makes a speciality of DBT, I at once determined it to be pretty effective. I started out sharing it with other human beings in my life, and I've discovered lots through my enjoy, sizeable research, and thru others sharing their memories with me. I don't know where I might be without DBT, but the amount of improvement I definitely have made inside the usage of DBT practices is surely tremendous to me and to my circle of relatives and buddies.

With a social tension sickness, it's far not unusual for humans to deny, cover or attempt more than one treatments for years without a remedy. I tried an entire lot of various topics too. I idea I modified into a out of region reason, and I in reality believed my tension become untreatable and I would possibly need to stay with debilitating, painful, and existence-changing tension all of the time. Honestly, I want to shout out to simply all of us who pays interest, "You are not on my own! Lots of human beings are suffering from comparable memories, however in reality everybody can alternate all that via the usage of using incorporating DBT into their existence!"

You can observe and exercising DBT with experts, pals, and/or own family members, but in the end it'll probably be your personal ardour and practice that will help you be your authentic, unafraid, formidable, and super self. Yes, I apprehend DBT received't make me otherwise you a high-quality man or woman however it will help us get to be had and make and study from our private errors (no longer our fears) and get hold of, forgive, and no longer determine ourselves so we are able to have a lifetime of annoying conditions, joys, screw ups, and successes!

So simply, in case you're whatever like me, I understand you want to recollect on this for yourself in advance than you placed the art work in... so, right right right here are a few real assets and studies that my father and I really have researched for ourselves and for you as properly.

Christian A Webb and his colleagues finished a have a look at in 2016 to conclude that the development of DBT talents will possibly reduce anxiety symptoms (Webb, n.D.).

A study at York University investigated which feelings (anger, worry, guilt, despair) decrease with DBT and whether or not or now not or no longer tension troubles moderate the ones effects. They concluded that DBT reduces numerous precise feelings, and anxiety troubles are possibly to facilitate the impact of worry, shame, and disappointment (Fitzpatrick, n.D.).

A check with the aid of Andrada D Neascsiu of Duke University Medical Center located that DBT-ST is a promising treatment for emotional dysregulation for anxiety (Neacsiu, n.D.).

So, what makes DBT this form of a achievement treatment technique for social tension you ask? It's DBT's capability to mix a number of the most scientifically tested coping mechanisms right into a unmarried powerful remedy. Three distinct factors make it artwork so nicely:

DBT is cognitive-based totally definitely. This manner that it allows you parent thoughts, ideals, and evaluations that aid on your belief of life; these may be healthful, extraordinary thoughts and/or terrible, nerve-racking ones. It creates belief styles that assist you emerge as privy to unhelpful highbrow patterns and boom one-of-a-kind tactics which is probably focused on growing excellent answers.

DBT is solution and guide-focused: It permits you revel in aware about your particular competencies and talents so that you can build on them to be the very awesome model of your self in the course of your life.

DBT is cooperative. It goes beyond theoretical thoughts and requires actual exercise. It encourages contact between you and great people, permitting you to exercise and increase social problem-fixing talents.

PROS AND CONS OF DBT

This is how one teenager we shared this with defined his enjoy with DBT:

"I changed into normally this shy child, a conventional introvert. The toughest a part of handling social anxiety become university. Because I come to be involved about my body form, I by no means felt confident inside the way I seemed. I felt like humans have been judging my weight, and that made me additionally experience like they have been judging what I became ingesting. At lunch, there were more than one specifically suggest, silly classmates who made fun of what I have become ingesting, evaluating it to what they had been ingesting. Their remarks overwhelmed me. All I should do end up withdraw and fear ingesting spherical different kids my age even extra.

"Even at the same time as a number of the children in my college institution grew up, and I didn't get picked on as an lousy lot, my tension stayed the identical, right into excessive college. It wasn't simply consuming both, as I changed into given more freedom, I located that taking public transportation, going out for meals with others, attending events in which there can be plenty of humans, putting out with friends, and having to make indicates in beauty have been all topics I feared. I even have become the sufferer of the 'spotlight impact,' which brought approximately me to feel hyper-self-aware of myself and the way I acted in social situations.

"When Hailey instructed me approximately her social tension and struggles, I modified into stunned. I couldn't take transport of as true with she modified into like me. We talked lots, and she or he instructed me approximately DBT. It has in fact helped me counteract the horrible automated mind that have been randomly wandering around in my head for years. I'm surprised at how one among a kind I revel in and am. Within a couple of months, my whole thoughts-set changed. I have become a real believer in DBT and specifically in myself. In reality, perhaps you could say DBT helped me recognize and consider in myself for the primary time ever. For me, 'misery tolerance' is the maximum useful of the four DBT abilties.

"The method come to be smooth, however it wasn't very easy. When I first commenced, it felt daunting due to the fact there are such plenty of factors to do not forget. Sometimes, I felt pressured and that might reason me to lose motivation. I was trying to teach myself to react in reality in any other case than I generally would in complicated conditions. I should pressure myself to face my feelings and recollect of them till the preliminary panic would in all likelihood vanish. Once I were given used to this device with DBT, I felt the enhance. Now, I revel in assured in nearly any situation. Not because of the reality I don't ever experience disturbing, however due to the reality I recognise how to take care of the ones feelings so I can do what I want to do. It's now not a magic, one-time tablet, however the greater I practice, the more automated my new responses end up. Bottom line is, it seems like my brain and body are starting to artwork with and for me in place of towards me."

Research and our personal stories have satisfied us that DBT is one of the outstanding techniques to assist humans deal with tension. However, as with something in life, DBT has easy and hard additives. It's vital to be privy to the ones, so right right here's our listing.

Easy:

DBT is evidence-based totally absolutely honestly. It's been significantly studied as alternatively powerful and it's scientifically showed every antidotally and through the use of examined length device to restrict anxiety and beautify the splendid of existence for human beings previously recognized with tension issues.

The machine are powerful strategies for reinforcing self-self notion and self-recognize.

DBT consists of strain manage strategies. This is specifically useful for staying calm within the direction of critical intervals.

DBT has a very immoderate crowning glory price in comparison to terrific remedy strategies. This way that those who start DBT live with it. A excessive final touch charge is an oblique marker of fulfillment.

DBT works remarkable for teens, but it moreover works for children and adults of any age. It is relevant for all gender identities, sexual orientations, and racial/ethnic backgrounds. It works for everybody!

Hard:

DBT isn't a short restore. It takes some time to apprehend and alter our deeply held physical and emotional beliefs, emotions, and reactions. Although alternate can also arise brief in a few instances, DBT won't produce its whole results with out time and practice.

It takes effort. DBT calls for a excessive diploma of willpower. You need to exercise the strategies and art work with distinctive people. The time you spend is flexible. You are on top of factors of at the same time as and the way you exercising, but the effects you enjoy will variety relying at the wonderful of your practice.

You should observe your learning in actual life as part of your whole determination to the treatment. This can revel in overwhelming in case you are doing it in your personal. If you sense caught, you'll want to recruit the assist of circle of relatives, a relied on pal, or a intellectual fitness employer (or all of them).

While exquisite elements of DBT are centered at the winning, others moreover require considering the beyond. Thinking approximately beyond traumas is often very frightening. Again, walking with a person who you can receive as authentic with and who can assist guide you thru that is often very useful.

Now which you recognize the professionals and cons, you can make your very non-public choice approximately trying this or now not. This is a remarkable time to start! After all, you have best worry to fear and your fear of worry is the only issue keeping you yet again!

Chapter 4: Mastering the Art of Witty Banter

Now which you have a number one information of social anxiety and DBT it's time to hobby on a few social competencies as a manner to throw your social anxiety proper out the window. Feeling assured in your ability as an appealing conversationalist is a key talent and no longer as tough to master as you may probable suppose. Think about it, if there can be one identifiable communique fashion that maximum young adults respond well to, it's witty banter.

You've seen that instructor, determine, or man or woman who income have an effect on with notable human beings with just a few seemingly handy quips. And you've watched the particularly charismatic child, who constantly appears to have a mild-hearted and clean-flowing observation, make buddies and look snug in even the maximum awkward situations. Turning to witty comments is a top notch manner for finding humor to your situation, lightening your mood, and growing first-rate strength for humans spherical to soak up and mirror again to you with endured or advanced positivity.

WHAT IS WITTY BANTER?

Witty banter is virtually an all-encompassing term for a conversational style that seeks to be fun, smart, and moderate-hearted. This approach to verbal exchange is helpful even as you want to bring life to your very own spirits at the same time as moreover helping installation rapport with people round you. Even one witty reaction in a social stumble upon is probably to spark greater engaging interactions.

To be clean, it's critical to understand that witty banter is in no manner insulting, rude, or condescending. Disparaging comments approximately yourself or exclusive humans are not some element however reasonably-priced and brief tactics to elicit responses. On the alternative hand, being excellent within the path of yourself and others is a examined path toward improving how others recognize you and the way you recognize yourself.

Witty banter may be brilliant and clean. It isn't approximately being a category clown or the center of interest. It's certainly approximately finding the amusing in conditions wherein special human beings might not see it proper away. Maybe you've heard the time period "fun police". These are the people who make it their business corporation to ensure no individual is taking detail in themselves. Think of yourself as the alternative. You are a "a laugh detective," fixing the puzzle of the way to take worrying, mundane, or dull social conditions and turn them into some thing you and others can experience.

WHY SHOULD YOU LEARN WITTY BANTER?

"I'm already laid low with social tension; how do you anticipate me to offer you witty banter?"

Remember that under your social tension lies fear of being judged, rejected, and/or embarrassed. Witty banter lets in you seem greater confident, and severa studies have proven that human beings are attracted to those people that appearance confident in ourselves. In fact, studies from the University of Sussex determined that if you are a assured character, human beings are extra inclined to accept as real with what you are saying and concur together with your ideals (Jake, n.D.).

The takeaway right here is that in case you give up on being a conversationalist, then it's going to stay tough to triumph over social tension. But, as you decide on your verbal exchange talents, you will get super responses from distinctive people. It's the ones increasingly great interactions with the intention to feed you with the self perception you want to experience better and higher approximately your capacity to give you witty banter and, in the long run, approximately yourself. Yes, it is probably a chunk of a fake it till you are making it method, however what the heck? It's moreover exercising that makes outstanding and so you've had been given this!

Technically, studying the art work of banter is ultimately tied to your improvisational abilties. For banter to be witty and now not insulting, you want to count on speedy underneath strain. Sounds hard? Don't worry; this isn't always a few component you want to be born with. Think of it this manner... improving competencies are a part of each unique difficulty of your lifestyles, and they will be superior thru workout. If you're a skilled musician, are you able to upload electricity to the critical rating? If you're an athlete, do you ever make a pass on the fly that a person with a whole lot a great deal less workout couldn't make? If you like video video games, are you able to see topics that a amateur doesn't recognize?

Whatever you're into, you may locate more examples of your functionality to be agile and witty with the property you workout. Your conversational wit is exercised and bolstered whilst you often banter with human beings you take shipping of as actual with.

It gained't take prolonged and soon you'll realise you are saying clever topics extra frequently. Doing this may be a laugh for you and others. It will assist beautify interactions and emotions with human beings round you, and it will assist to keep to enhance your self belief.

Here's a chunk example. My sister and my mother and father have been speaking approximately her birthday party and there was a few anxiety about how I could probable react to having such plenty of one among a kind young adults (some of whom I like and others not a lot) in our residence for a massive party. When my dad and mom asked who changed into coming, she began to list the names. I may additionally need to appearance my dad getting involved because of the fact the list grew longer and my mother began to argue that our house wasn't large enough to host all of the ones people. At first, I honestly sat there and discreetly pretended that I wasn't listening. Then, with a deep breath, I referred to as up my witty banter, and my exercising kicked in. I acted as although I had just come to be aware of what they have been discussing.

"Oh nice, I'll be there too."

"I already knew that," my sister responded.

"Yeah, and I forgot to say, around three and 4 of my friends might be coming too, of direction," I introduced, with a moderate smile and a small nod to the humor I have become adding to the speak.

She changed into a bit bowled over earlier than she and my parents commenced out to slowly piece together my funny tale.

"Really? No, they are now not. We have already got such severa..." she insisted.

"I'm joking; it's likely going to be six or seven," I answered with a giggle.

Ultimately, my shaggy dog tale dispelled the unwelcome tension they have been developing in a conversation that (sarcastically) have become about my social anxiety. It grow to be in addition fun considering that my family also can want to tell from my frame language and tone of voice that I in reality wasn't planning to ask a listing of my buddies to my sister's birthday celebration. They stopped bickering over it proper away, at the least inside the the front of me. Learning the way to exchange the dynamics of a situation is a handy dandy tool. Any organization will credit score rating and recognize you to your beauty and cunning if you may use banter to diffuse uncomfortable situations.

HOW TO BE A PRO AT BANTERING WITHOUT INSULTING OTHERS

The reason of banter is to have amusing for your self and the encompassing humans. It's in no way approximately undermining every body else. To be a high-quality comic story, it should be universally funny. Here are some realistic suggestions to help you draw near the skills of bantering.

Body language and Delivery: Think approximately my sister's birthday instance. It's not all approximately what you're saying, but moreover the manner you say it. Why is it that humans could make the identical humorous story, but one falls flat whilst the opportunity hits the mark? The solution commonly lies in frame language, voice tone, and shipping this is going past the phrases themselves. It become my mild smile and clean tone of voice that allow them understand a comic story is probably coming as quickly as I first interjected into the communication. It modified proper into a broader smile and fun that mounted the shaggy canine tale and opened the door for them to snicker too when I mockingly counseled that even extra people have been coming.

Most of our communication is non-verbal. We create the because of this of our phrases using little indicators, together with our frame posture, eye contact, facial expressions, and tone of voice. You recognize the vintage pronouncing, "A photograph is well certainly well worth 1000 words." Well, witty banter is ready your body language, growing an entire word image for whoever you are speaking with. These non-verbals don't ought to be large or over dramatic. Think of the energy you add in your communique thru simply curling your nostrils once more even as your parents say they will be making meals you don't like or the high first rate message you send whilst you sniff at the air even as they say they're getting geared up your chosen dinner. Even the most diffused non-verbals give a boost to your transport and the effect of your witty conversation.

Teasing: When you playfully tease a person, you are each offering them praise and putting in a task. This can create a fun pull-push dynamic. For example, hold in thoughts that you have been assigned to associate on a class task with someone who you understand to be popular in beauty but who you feel stressful about operating with while it's in truth the 2 of you together. Sure sufficient, there can be an inept silence that you would like to interrupt...

"Dude, you're hilarious...it's too horrible you're so dull at the same time as we're running on schoolwork collectively."

When you land a tease like this successfully, via way of adding a nice smile with the punchline it produces a a laugh reaction or response as opposed to persevering with the gloomy and awkward silence. This may moreover seem insulting without context, however with the right frame language and tone, this will open a large variety of a laugh conversations amongst individuals who are becoming pals. Make sure you reserve this form of excellent banter, for whilst you apprehend the person you're teasing is receptive to this shape of humor due to the truth a few human beings would probable find out it insulting. If they don't come up with the hey sign or appear standoffish, double down with a praise. "No kidding, I in reality scored on getting you as my associate. I recognize we are going to ace this!"

Thinking at the move: Bantering could require you to anticipate at the cross. Timing is the whole lot as you exercise your instant and spontaneous responses. It's useful to have a few jokes and one-liners concept out earlier that you can exercising and depend on as you continue to decorate this capability. To help keep away from looking scripted, try lightly guidance the communicate in a course in that you may likely utilize your line.

For example, if your business enterprise is speaking approximately a certainly tough elegance at college, you can wait till they talk about a mainly tough elegance or steer the verbal exchange via way of announcing "I've were given a trick for purchasing at once A's" earlier than you quip, "it's usimg a ruler."

If you've got got the possibility, take improv lessons as a manner to beautify bantering. Improv isn't always first-rate fun, however it additionally teaches you to roll with the punches that come at you. Improv teaches you a manner to adapt to what the opposite individual can provide in desire to trying to push a particular end. It's smooth to sense the tendency to want to overrate a statement in an try and decide if it'll probably be humorous. Practicing improv will assist you learn how to take into account your intuition, reply abruptly, and experience greater confident within the method. It's anywhere within the global. Improv will enhance your banter and your life.

TIMING IS EVERYTHING

Just like with each different talents, dashing into creating a humorous tale is a awful concept until you have got got got an concept as to how the people round you can reply. It's vital which you have a brilliant statistics of what's occurring round you and who's worried in the state of affairs.

Here is what a witty banter gadget seems like:

Perfect banter = spontaneous wondering + right frame language + fun tone + proper time

If you pass over out on one of these factors, there's a hazard that your banter may not hit its mark. Remember, in fact due to the truth some problem is humorous to you in a single second doesn't mean that it's going to probably be humorous to a person else or that it'll be appropriate in each different state of affairs. So you need to be careful about what you're announcing and to whom you are announcing it. Not genuinely absolutely everyone is open to your jokes, you apprehend. Avoid topics that have a tendency to be related to in particular sturdy values, ideals, and feelings. Steering smooth of topics like faith or politics is often a accurate concept and as an opportunity, choose out to consciousness on the more trivial matters that you pay interest humans make small talk approximately every day….Meals, a laugh sports, sports activities, and many others.

Chapter 5: A Guide to Charismatic Communication

Have you ever puzzled why a number of your friends seem extra assured than others? What traits outline them as being charismatic? Why are a number of your friends surely better at shooting an target market? The solution to the ones questions is critical to you. Having the aura to draw, attraction, and function an effect at the human beings round you can help you assemble conceitedness and self belief. And, bet what, vanity and self guarantee are very powerful antidotes to social tension.

UNDERSTANDING THE ART OF CHARISMATIC COMMUNICATION

Over 1000 participants took detail in a have a look at on aura accomplished through researchers from the University of Toronto. They located that air of mystery combines "affability" and "affect" (Tskhay, 2017).

Influence changed into described as having both leadership ability and a effective presence

Affability modified into described as being notable and handy.

In her cutting-edge-day day ebook, Cues: Master the Secret Language of Charismatic Communication, creator Vanessa Van Edwards talks about the era within the back of charisma and gives insights into a manner to beautify have an effect on and affability.

Her ebook talks about the 4 styles of cues identifiable with social capabilities. Cues are simply indicators to be aware about. A cue well-knownshows someone's feelings within the course of an settlement, an concept, in any other case you. You gets tips approximately upcoming conduct at the same time as you're aware of those cues. In fact, maximum interpersonal issues we are facing typically rise up at the equal time as we fail to observe the cues that unique human beings are giving or we don't supply the proper cues to others about how we sense. Incorrect interpretation of various human beings's signs and symptoms or sending incomplete alerts yourself reasons misunderstandings approximately essential feelings or intentions. So what are the ones cues?

Verbal cues (an apparent one)

Non-verbal cues

Vocal cues

Imagery cues

Most people generally tend to popularity an entire lot of hobby on verbal cues and permit the alternative three cues to live underrated. Mastering the art work of air of mystery calls as a way to be aware of all four cues.

Charismatic human beings are commonly confident, or at the least they may project self assure. Having the capability to speak with any luck is essential. But it is not sufficient to go back backpedal as assured clearly in conversations. You need to exercise exuding self belief through one-of-a-type social cues as properly. The self assurance you task for your presence, voice, and appearance will inspire others to experience the equal way approximately you. This isn't about being conceited or conceited. Truly charismatic teenagers have a healthful revel in of self belief, tempered with humility, that stems from being privy to and training their social queues through the years.

The capability to get alongside properly with extraordinary humans and to help make other human beings experience comfortable is a exceptional feature of a charismatic individual. This takes capability in having the ability to call emotions that you may be feeling. Charismatic individuals are proper at expressing their actual emotions in a non violent but sincere way and moreover at information how human beings spherical them are feeling. It isn't always first-rate about the terms which is probably being spoken, it's additionally about the manner you venture and react to nonverbal, vocal, and imagery cues.

Charisma includes actual frame language and an active, passionate, and enthusiastic communication fashion. It technique projecting a first rate outlook, being upbeat, humble, and grateful, and being subtly influential enough to gain the hobby and agree with of others. Remember, human beings like folks who are interested in and prefer them, so questions of hobby and compliments skip an prolonged way in maintaining these conversations going. Of path, this is all overwhelming if you are a teen with social tension. But grasp in there; just like with one-of-a-kind talents, air of mystery is constructed through workout, and we've got a few simple ideas with the intention to attempt on this bankruptcy.

HABITS OF CHARISMATIC COMMUNICATOR

Sure, a few humans appear to be truely charismatic, however maximum humans examine those skills through the years. Here are a few techniques that will help you experience more charismatic in every interaction. First, it's vital to recognize which you are getting to know to increase a trustworthy communique fashion that encourages and inspires others. The motive is to help set up sincere relationships with others and recognise their dreams whilst respecting your non-public desires. There are a few conduct that make charismatic people exquisite communicators. Let's discover a number of them:

Making others the center of enchantment: Some people expect that air of secrecy is ready displaying your developments to others, but it's genuinely the exact opposite. If you appearance carefully, charismatic human beings speak extra about others than themselves. Usually, they prioritize asking questions over expressing critiques and that they have engaged listeners whilst one-of-a-kind people are speakme. They are unique at making others enjoy important with the aid of giving their complete hobby to whoever they're speaking with.

Here is one in each of my all-time favourite costs approximately air of mystery:

"Charisma is not virtually pronouncing hi there. It's dropping what you are doing to mention good day" - Robert Brault (Sonaike, n.D.).

When you deal with others in a manner that makes them revel in unique, they'll truely appreciate your efforts and treat you with specific consideration, too.

Here's any other high-quality trick… Complimenting a mutual friend within the returned in their again is a powerful way to earn bear in mind every with the man or woman you are complimenting and the person you're sharing the communication with.

Being Optimistic: Charismatic humans are appropriate at looking for the pleasant in the whole lot. They venture a effective thoughts-set and their actions display sturdy resilience. Negativity has a bent to attract special terrible people, however negativity is human beings repellant to the people you really need to be round. In the clever phrases of considered considered one in every of my favored teachers, "Nobody likes a mope". Although positivity is in call for, it has an inclination to be unusual, specifically for teens. Look round, humans spend a number of time complaining. And, maximum conversations live on a whole lot of terrible stuff. That's probably because it feels a whole lot less complicated to agree and most human beings find out it much less difficult to speak about what they don't like instead of what they do like.

Seriously, would now not or now not it is much less complex to invite every other youngster in the occasion that they hate polka music as an lousy lot as you do or if they love your selected musician as masses as you do? But, in reality, that's handiest a horrific addiction. Negativity isn't always what people honestly revel in. People want to be uplifted by way of exceptional remarks and moves. People need to be around charismatic people due to the reality they're extra exciting and upbeat about maximum events.

Being superb at storytelling: Charismatic people normally seem to have interesting testimonies to inform; their compelling imaginative and prescient and communication style every play roles in this. They can efficiently deliver their message thru being excessive and/or including humor as needed to maintain the attention of their audience. The trick proper here is that a charismatic man or woman realizes that it's not as plenty about the content material fabric as it is approximately their style of transport. Their open, snug frame language, which includes hundreds of eye touch, allows make this viable. They preserve a watch out for cues and responses from the humans they'll be talking with and adjust their tone and fashion as essential.

You will find out that paying attention to the same tale from a charismatic individual might not experience much like others who don't speak with that self perception, enthusiasm, or rhythm. I believe that exercising makes terrific, so at this component, if I certainly have a story I want to percent with a person, I now and again exercise it within the replicate first, to make certain I experience assured inside the shipping. Am I mumbling, or am I handing over It like a rock large name?

TIPS FOR CHARISMATIC COMMUNICATION

The one actual detail of being a charismatic teen is to undertaking self belief. But your social tension feels love it hinders your capability to appear assured, proper? So, is the idea of aura best a delusion for disturbing young adults? No, not at all. Here we cross once more, "Fake it, until you are making it." That is exactly what you may do and high quality, you have got had been given this!

Confidence and air of thriller paintings in a loop, complementing each exclusive. It all genuinely takes workout. Like the day my cousin requested me if I favored to play frisbee with him. I hadn't ever completed that earlier than, so I didn't revel in confident in my functionality to throw or seize, and I doubt I projected a number of charisma as I walked out onto the grass with him. But it didn't take lengthy for me to get the draw close of it. Pretty speedy, I have become acting greater comfortable, even feeling more assured, and before I knew it, I even located myself showboating with a piece of air of thriller after a in particular "fortunate" seize.

If you workout your charisma enough, you will in the end expand the vital self notion, at the manner that will help you be even greater charismatic. This is what I did and due to the reality I'm probably not that distinctive from you, you may do it, too.

Confidence > Charisma (You begin faking it from proper right here) > Confidence > More Charisma

Pay interest to the human beings round you. As you try this, you'll be aware that people are inquisitive about the folks that are most comfy with themselves. This degree of ease comes from real statistics and perception in each their very personal value, the fee of the message they are speakme, and the charge they have got in others.

So here are a few guidelines to fake your manner thru (and into) aura and to encompass your actual price, the fee of your verbal exchange, and your appreciation of others.

Be enthusiastic and lively: What makes a amazing conversationalist incredible? Their presence. The pleasant thing to do in an effort to be a part of deeply with a person is to be clearly immersed in a verbal exchange. The slight on your eyes, the care for your voice, and the satisfaction and conviction in your body language will talk for themselves. You need to be confident (or at the least appear so). I had a math instructor who as quickly as suggested me, "You don't should pay interest in my magnificence, you best want to faux which you are." The equal is proper here. You don't need to apprehend all of the right topics to say, you genuinely want to be engaged.

Remember that no individual is interested by a lethargic and coffee-power individual due to the fact they drain the life out of others. Be the alternative. Pour life into human beings via your body language and your enthusiasm. If you don't understand some thing about the problem or are pressured, truely ask questions.

Embrace emotional intelligence: This one is a no brainer. All charismatic human beings are emotionally clever. Yes, they all. Being emotionally practical manner being privy to your private feelings and having the functionality to pick out and manipulate them. Developing this talent has the brought gain of creating you more talented in data different human beings's emotions and knowledge the way to reply to them.

You might be conscious that charismatic humans are aware of their very very own feelings. They also are tremendous at expressing themselves in a smooth and non-emotional way. This is one of the subjects that makes them stand out. When a person brazenly stocks how they revel in, with out performing out their emotions in a bad manner, different people round them moreover enjoy stimulated to do the identical. This opens the door to help create deeper connections and shape large relationships.

Avoid Reactionary Communication: This too requires being emotionally smart. Being charismatic is not quality about speaking approximately fun subjects, it is also about studying to address difficult conversations. You want to stay grounded and no longer reply to heightened emotions. It's a hard ability to study (maximum adults nonetheless war with this one), however it comes right down to in reality acting cool underneath pressure. Similarly, it's also approximately staying cool while unique people are in a reactive country round you. Slowing down and definitely listening are critical strategies here.

Show hobby in fantastic people: Who does no longer love to talk approximately themselves? Everyone does. Everyone also loves folks who permit them to speak about themselves. Make other people sense favored via using shining your mild on them. Listen to what others have to inform you. You can take this in addition with the aid of asking the proper questions. When you ask questions, other people pay interest which you are interested by them. Nobody enjoys a one-manner conversation to preserve the ball moving among you and others.

I realise what you're in all likelihood wondering: "It's less difficult stated than completed, Hailey." I honestly agree. But, it is also actual that being a charismatic communicator is not rocket generation, and assuming it's too difficult for you isn't accepting your self, it's accepting mediocrity. The nice element you want to grow to be a charismatic teenager is to trust it is feasible (and then preserve trying until it's far).

Chapter 6: Improving Your People Skills

You recognize that toddler that looks snug speaking with each person? Yes, I advocate absolutely everyone. It doesn't depend if it's a instructor, parents, or perhaps specific young adults, they will be seasoned at talking with absolutely everyone. You possibly want you had a piece of that magic and feature puzzled how they do it. How are they suitable at talking with all people? In this bankruptcy, we communicate approximately this very trait: human beings abilties. Perhaps thru the give up of this financial ruin, you'll have a number of the ones magic hints up your sleeves, too.

WHAT ARE PEOPLE SKILLS?

People skills, additionally called easy skills, are interpersonal talents that help you effectively communicate with extraordinary humans. In one among a type contexts, they're known as communication, teamwork, trouble-fixing, leadership, and different comparable abilties.

People skills are reachable in every putting, which includes your private home, faculty, university, social gatherings, non-public relationships, or workplace. Some of your pals may genuinely be natural at this. You might be conscious them handling conflicts between pals, making purchases from carriers appearance smooth, and building rapport with strangers. But for people with social anxiety, the ones same interactions are frequently hard. Don't fear. I became that way too. But I've learned to workout my manner of growing the vital abilties for building and preserving people competencies.

THE LIKABILITY QUOTIENT

Before discussing how you can increase people capabilities, permit us to communicate approximately the likability quotient. What makes a few human beings greater likable than others? Likability is a key difficulty close to social interactions. Whether you are trying to make buddies or be invited to occasions, likability will take you in that you need to move. It is a trait that attracts humans inside the direction of you, like a magnet. To be a people man or woman, you want to be likable.

When you're preferred via others, social interplay becomes plenty less complicated. You will revel in extra confident and your vanity can be better whilst people enjoy your presence. People with likable attributes are people with great people talents. So what form of character does anybody like?

There is a famous announcing through John Maxwell:

"Greatness is described by way of the usage of way of what a person offers, now not by means of manner of what they get."

(ERIN URBA, 2018)

Likability comes all of the way all of the way right down to having an enough thoughts-set. Basically, due to this you experience like you have got the thoughts-set of giving first on the way to acquire. In order to attain, you will discover ways to deliver in abundance.

Give compliments: Everyone values the feeling that includes a nice praise. But you don't need to come back off as insincere. It's crucial to be focused and set off to your technique. Be searching for specific people's interests. For instance, if you see that they have new shoes, you may praise them the primary time you see them. Or, if they may be into gaming, you can reward them on their talents. If they are appropriate at instructors, honor them with a compliment approximately a excessive test score. Best of all, if a person allows you, say "thank you" and praise them for the selection. If there is a person you want to be buddies with, attempt complimenting them to one of a type humans. Complimenting a person behind their again is a powerful way to influence them, in addition to the people you percentage the compliment with.

Give away time: Time is valuable. When you actively proportion a while with others, you offer them the winning of a shared revel in. This is a beneficial gift. Listening to and valuing some unique character's angle is one of the greatest conduct you can boom. Very few topics are as worthwhile as while someone takes the time to invite approximately our lives, how we revel in, our opinions, and our beliefs. This is a extraordinary gift to present to others.

Give away kindness: Be high-quality, the sector can always use a chunk extra… well, "exceptional". Sincere relationships can most effective be constructed at the cornerstone of kindness. Nobody loves a self-targeted snob who exceptional thinks about their very own pursuits. Be the opposite, be kind to absolutely everyone, anywhere and everywhere.

Your social anxiety will enhance by way of manner of your giving. Giving is a manner of becoming a more desired character on your network and circle. Others will experience your kindness, a few returning it with their very personal kindness, and in the long run building you up at the same time. That's how the offer-to-receive principle works! When you enjoy favored and favored, you could revel in like you've got had been given the strength to speak more correctly with out giving in in your underlying social tension.

HOW TO DEVELOP PEOPLE SKILLS

As a teenager experiencing SAD, the idea of running on people abilities development can sound too educational and enjoy daunting. But it's the ones treasured abilities in an effort to be the critical thing in your fulfillment and open doorways as you're making deeper connections and perhaps (in case you are ever involved) in the end address management roles as well.

Here are some easy topics to hold in thoughts for developing the ones abilties:

Relate to others: It's vital to connect to others and their conditions at a non-public degree. The nice manner to do this is thru using sharing not unusual pursuits that the opportunity individual unearths relatable. Connecting with anybody of any age is feasible if you could find relatable subjects to talk about. Often, the ones commonplace pastimes convey you inside the route of different humans. I need to look for small clues to discover common interests. Like a detective, I task myself to look and pay attention for any clues about a subject that I must enjoy exploring greater with the character I'm meeting. For instance, I like cats. So, if I see that they have a picture of a cat on their mobile telephone or if I pay attention them talk approximately a cat with a person else, I get the chance to invite them if they like cats which opens the opportunity for me to pay attention them percentage their hobby in cats.

Patience with others: It's continuously a splendid exercise to take note that you don't recognize what every special man or woman has happening in their life.

I take into account the time I have become feeling worrying approximately having a communique with a boy I was paired with on a category project. I didn't realise hundreds approximately him, and his response turn out to be underwhelming once I attempted to apply the icebreakers I had practiced. He failed to seem in any respect inquisitive about having a verbal exchange. Little did I understand that it had not anything to do with me in any respect. It wasn't until later that I located he have turn out to be going via a few quite heavy non-public issues at domestic.

You want to be patient with relationships. After all, I do no longer like feeling judged via other humans if I'm a bit awkward because of my social tension. Who is aware of, the opportunity character you're speaking with might be stricken by social anxiety too. Don't judge different human beings by using the use of their first response. Patience for the way extraordinary people are reacting is an indication of your personal humility and recognize for their barriers. Just with the useful resource of honoring them with this staying power, you open the door to greater bear in mind, know-how, and apprehend. In my example, by using way of the use of allowing the verbal exchange to expand at a slower pace simply so the boy felt unjudged and had time to get cushty with me, we slowly became friends. That's how we advanced a relationship wherein he depended on me sufficient to inform me about what have become going on at home, and the way I won a chum to percentage some of my secrets and techniques and techniques as nicely. In truth, he have become one of the first teens I advised approximately my social anxiety.

Be susceptible: Vulnerability is one of the important additives of a dating that really doesn't seem to get enough credit score. The word vulnerability doesn't advise susceptible or pathetic and it's clearly not about being focused on terrible matters. It's approximately authentically sharing your values, your evaluations, and what makes you... you.

Being prone isn't commonly advocated. It feels very complicated because we want to challenge self notion and vulnerability can on occasion experience in comparison to that self belief. But, it's clearly without a doubt separate. What it manner is that in area of overcompensating or attempting hard to win someone over via being "pleasant," you're allowing your self to be confident in what I like to name "ideal imperfections." When you permit humans see the real you, you create an open environment that permits huge connections with others.

That's comprehensible. This is due to the truth, as humans, we typically try to behave in a manner that we think will make anybody like us. Being susceptible approach deliberately identifying to permit human beings the danger to get to recognise the real you, and to choose for themselves within the occasion that they need to determine, be your friend or now not. In my mind, vulnerability is actually some other phrase for honesty and authenticity. Here are some actionable steps to harness the power of vulnerability:

It's properly enough to understand, and to speak approximately, topics which you preference had been precise for your life. Everyone makes errors and screw ups are only failures if we don't have a look at from them. Being sincere approximately the beyond and open to change in the future is a trademark of vulnerability and success.

Taking obligation for yourself and in no way blaming certainly one of a kind human beings or activities. You understand that the handiest trouble you manipulate is your self. It's as an lousy lot as you to be liable to the idea that in case you want topics to be first-rate, you can create that route ahead for yourself.

Expressing the way you enjoy. Vulnerability is set sharing your emotions with different humans round you. This can be very simply one of a kind from asking them to be chargeable for the manner you experience (see the personal obligation component above). It's surely about no longer protecting the manner you experience and being honest with yourself and the people you are with.

Be empathetic: Empathy is the ability to understand the feelings of others. In the same way that it feels accurate to supply different people apprehend you, it's furthermore crucial to try to recognize others. Everyone has specific perspectives, ideas, values, ideals, and studies that reason them to really precise. To enjoy a incredible relationship, you need to have empathy to understand who humans are and the way they experience. So how do you exercise empathy?

Listen to understand, no longer to respond. Imagine what it would feel want to be them

Ask clarifying questions. As you consider their enjoy, ask them to proportion in extra element.

Don't decide or offer recommendation. This isn't approximately you sharing your perspective, it's about reading as loads as you may approximately theirs

You're not a mind reader and also you'll never actually recognise what's happening in every different individual's head, but you may exercise empathy, and you may have a look at that your ability to narrate, apprehend, and really be part of will enhance. And, as you connect with others, your very personal anxiety will disappear.

Chapter 7: Putting an End to Social Anxiety for Good

Since you've take a look at this a ways, you have already got a few extraordinary system for subjects to workout. But as someone who has lengthy long gone thru all this, I apprehend how the priority of social interactions that you are regardless of the fact that going via lingers. While the art work of communique comes naturally to a few, we (the socially traumatic young adults) recognize how tough it really is.

In this financial ruin, we take your communique abilities up a notch. We're going even similarly to offer you the machine to use to grow to be a strong communicator.

UNDERSTANDING VERBAL AND NON-VERBAL COMMUNICATION

Communication is product of all of the actions a person does at the equal time as talking with others. It is a normal process of telling, listening, and comprehending terms, and seen and audio cues. Communication, as you may understand (sure, proper here comes the dull factor from my dad again), may be divided into distinguished instructions:

Verbal: This is while phrases are used to carry facts. It is composed of each written and spoken communication. It consists of government memos, letters, organisation newsletters, e-mails, internet pages, bulletin board posts, manuals, in-man or woman conferences, speeches and shows, and videoconferences. (Suparna, n.D.)

Non-Verbal: This refers to the alternate of information via body language, gestures, facial emotions, created region, and one of a kind nonverbal cues. (Suparna, n.D.)

Although verbal conversation is important, maximum verbal exchange is simply non-verbal communication. Since I started out using, I want to reflect onconsideration on verbal conversation as a avenue signal and non-verbal verbal exchange as the whole thing else happening on the road. Like, a pace restriction sign is obviously important, and at the same time, I need to be privy to what percentage of different cars are on the street, the climate, visibility, go with the flow of web web page web site visitors, homes, intersections, and pedestrians... There's loads to take in. All that stuff informs me as to how speedy it's strong for me to force.

Non-verbal verbal exchange offers us most of the vital clues approximately what one of a kind humans are thinking and feeling. Effective verbal conversation is important for success in non-public and professional relationships. And similar to the antique pronouncing approximately a photo speakme a thousand terms, it's our non-verbal cues—additionally referred to as frame language—that communicate louder than phrases.

Whether you understand it or now not, you constantly deliver and gather nonverbal cues even as interacting with every body. Your posture, tone of voice, quantity of eye contact, gestures, and super minor information carry vital messages. These little records should make others experience comfortable, gather don't forget, and trap them to you, or they will worsen, baffle, and sabotage what you are attempting to say. These indicators preserve even while you aren't interacting in any respect. Even while someone is certainly repute within the front of you, they will be although speaking a few difficulty to you non-verbally.

One day, my dad came to me and mentioned going on a street experience. I turn out to be excited due to the reality I idea we were going to move someplace I idea might be an interestIng adventure. I idea I modified into going to have fun with my own family. But then he knowledgeable me that a number of his pals from paintings and their families had been going to go in this journey too. Well, the demanding infant I have become, I did now not want to go on a revel in with a big business organisation of humans I didn't apprehend. I have become dissatisfied, however I did no longer say a phrase to my dad because of the reality he seemed to be genuinely looking earlier to it.

But like most terrific dads in the global, they understand a manner to select out up on nonverbal cues from their daughters. He requested me if I changed into feeling stressful about it and he told me that it turned into adequate to again out. I like sharing this tale due to the fact that modified into the instantaneous I found out how excellent it feels to have someone for your existence recognize what you are attempting to speak, even on the equal time as you aren't the use of phrases to specific your feelings.

I suppose it's honestly exciting that every now and then what we are saying and suggest to mention with our frame language will have absolutely high-quality meanings. Watch out for this to ensure that you truly apprehend what is being communicated to you. It is critical to understand this reality because of the fact humans need to be heard, and they normally recognize it whilst you be conscious the data in their frame language as a huge a part of how they talk. It is likewise crucial to deliver the right alerts when you are interacting with someone. If you say one trouble and act otherwise, your listeners will experience which you are being dishonest.

HOW TO IMPROVE NON-VERBAL COMMUNICATION

Non-verbal conversation calls for your entire attention. This is known as energetic listening. If you're distracted thru an out of doors event or considering responding, you'll leave out out at the nonverbal cues your pals are displaying. You can have hassle knowledge the complexities of what humans attempt to mention if you aren't the usage of all your senses to get keep of their communication. The 3 essential factors of nonverbal communique are to govern the strain that includes it, increase your emotional popularity, and be actually present within the second.

"But I locate it difficult to even start a communication; how do you count on me to attention on my and exclusive people's non-verbal cues all the time?....."

I get you. The anxiety impairs your functionality for all communication, each verbal and non-verbal. It develops more possibilities to misread others, supply off dubious or unwelcoming non-verbal signs, and have interaction in knee-jerk reactions. Again, the first-class way to comprehend non-verbal communique is through exercising. It received't seem in a single day, however you will get there.

Remember, if you enjoy uncomfortable, you don't have to leap right proper right into a verbal exchange. Before you're taking the plunge right right into a talk, take a minute to accumulate your composure. You'll continuously address the entirety higher whilst you experience emotionally balanced.

To supply your non-verbal symptoms and symptoms successfully, you want to be privy to your emotions and the manner they have got an impact in your complete frame. You moreover want to enjoy prepared to take a look at one-of-a-kind human beings's body language and understand their sentiments. This is wherein emotional attention comes into play. You can also experience tempted to say something that isn't consistent with the way you actually experience, however your nonverbal cues will normally provide you with away. Instead of preventing the internal battle, you may have more control over your thoughts and moves in case you examine to hook up with the feelings which you are experiencing in advance than you begin speaking.

Once you have got got have been given evolved the skills to apprehend and manage the ones in any other case traumatic feelings, your non-verbal verbal exchange will in reality enhance. Here are a few small suggestions to make you a hold close at non-verbal communication:

Pay attention to inconsistencies: What humans say want to be supported by way of non-verbal clues. Does the speaker appear dissatisfied even though they're saying they aren't? Take a collective take a look at all of the non-verbal cues. Do not interpret too much from a single nonverbal trace or gesture. Take phrase in their body language, tone of voice, gestures, and eye contact. When you have a look at the entire image together, do their nonverbal signs and symptoms manual—or contradict—what they are asserting verbally?

Maintain cushty eye touch: Eye contact is the primary issue to help you hook up with particular human beings. This is not similar to staring, but don't keep away from eye contact. Meeting someone's gaze shows that you are in fact concerned and giving them your undivided interest.

Maintain an open frame posture: Keep a impartial stance. For example, if your palms are crossed throughout your frame, you would possibly appearance (or genuinely be) closed off or shielding within the course of various humans. Open body language way that you are receptive to talking, listening, and connecting.

Avoid Fidgeting: Yes, certain, I have been there. You enjoy tempted to fidget, specially even as you're having an uncomfortable verbal exchange. But this may be very distracting for the other individual. Also, it is able to provide the unintentional impact that you are bored or which you simply don't want to talk.

Avoid searching at your cellphone: The traditional current-day problem. Do now not look at your phone even as speakme to someone. This certainly, all the time, shows you're tired of taking note of what the opportunity man or woman is announcing and that your cellphone is more critical to you.

These nonverbal cues, while mixed, will help you talk a good buy more successfully. Most frequently, what you specific via your body language is greater critical than what you are saying. But I can't strain this enough. These are conduct and it requires a variety of exercise to place into effect these into your daily conversations.

IMPROVING YOUR SELF-ESTEEM AND SILENCING THAT INNER CRITIC

Since you're reading this ebook, I'm positive you need to feel confident approximately your self. But just like anybody, that evil inner critic of yours remains in search of to maintain you again. It nevertheless fills your thoughts with self-doubt, lack of self belief, and fear. Self-esteem is the notion we've had been given approximately ourselves. Everyone has periods of feeling down or having problem believing in themselves, however it's even more persistent in teens experiencing social tension.

Low shallowness usually can be traced again to some of our terrible reviews, but it moreover has a bent to sneak up into the winning and hit you every time, normally while we least assume it. Social media specifically performs a massive function in this. Perhaps you scroll down and word your buddies doing splendid in teachers, having a hit relationships, looking for new expensive stuff, and so on. Your shallowness plummets. You begin questioning why you're lagging in the back of your pals in those methods. It's clean to begin wondering your life options and begin feeling that you aren't pinnacle enough at this, that, or the other element. These varieties of comparisons and associated emotions should make your already present day social anxiety even worse.

Since social media has surrounded us, our belief of ourselves may be very relative. Every time you get right of entry to your feed, your conceitedness is vulnerable to taking every different hit. This is due to the truth social media is an open invitation to assess your lifestyles to others. Your inner critic then effortlessly activates your shortcomings in assessment to others, in region of recognizing all the accomplishments you have achieved and the things that make you specific.

It's easy to get conceitedness and self assurance combined up. They aren't the identical. There is a incredible line between the 2. Your vanity impacts the manner you word yourself. In assessment, your self-self assurance dictates how you understand your very very personal skills and talents.

You can increase yourself-self perception via walking for your competencies and using past records relevant to the paintings. In assessment, excessive self-self guarantee but awful arrogance can also quit result at the same time as you receive as actual with for your capability to perform some factor however doubt your actual fee.

I had an high-quality buddy developing up who appeared to have numerous conceitedness troubles. Her father, who she manifestly seemed up to, become by no means a totally best man, and he continuously criticized her. On the other hand, her mom can also need to strive her wonderful to present her compliments, but most of these had been pretty shallow and no longer based totally on her real achievements.

As she had been given older, she started to get extra crucial of herself and he or she had trouble getting obsessed with the huge accomplishments she changed into having in her lifestyles (even some issue small like celebrating an tremendous check score). In hindsight now, it's smooth for me to peer how this manifested as social anxiety later as she grew into her teenager years.

She felt insufficient and took criticism very in my view. Due to her social tension, she did now not in shape in with any commercial enterprise organization at college, and maximum of her school breaks and weekends were spent with me. Even despite the fact that she and I had an extended-lasting courting, inspite of me she in no way felt comfortable in social situations. This lack of self-esteem persisted all the way thru faculty.

But while she modified into round 18, on the point of graduate from immoderate university and head into college, she commenced running on her self guarantee and shallowness. I watched her closely and saw how she transformed her lifestyles from an stressful younger youngster into someone who thrives in nearly any new state of affairs. To me, she is a living belief, and I simply have masses to research from her. Here are some topics that she shared with me which have helped her boom:

Stop being a humans pleaser: People-captivating conduct brings down your vanity because of the reality you're constantly thinking about subjects so one can make others happy in location of prioritizing your non-public nicely-being. People with low-self confidence generally have a tendency to are searching for validation from unique people and regularly have hassle announcing No. They prioritize different humans's wishes above their very own. Although being supportive and beneficial while you could is often a remarkable thing, in case you base your charge on how a wonderful deal you are captivating one in every of a type humans, your arrogance will in the end go through. Honor your private boundaries, cope with your self, and help others in approaches that uplift each of you.

Get out of that comfort zone: Most humans are continuously searching for techniques of staying of their comfort place. If you don't experience cushty assembly new people, it's easy to try to discover strategies of warding off those kinds of interactions. But recognize this, not whatever brilliant ever occurs in our comfort region. So get out of it once in a while. Personally, I just like the announcing, "get comfortable being uncomfortable". It's funny to me, and it's an top notch reminder to push myself as soon as I understand there's an possibility that I might probably revel in if I do.

My buddy, in her quest to growth self-esteem, tried her remarkable to cope with specific possibilities that she as quickly as idea had been now not viable. For instance, she went directly to now not pleasant be part of a membership in university, however to preserve herself out as a frontrunner in that organization, catching the attention of every pupil in the school. The excessive college buddy I knew might by no means have even idea of doing a little element like that. But whilst she ultimately attempted it, she determined that she turn out to be outstanding at organizing sports activities sports and assisting to make the club a laugh for everyone who had joined. She have become a exquisite chief!

I'm certain it modified into difficult for her to speak up once they were requesting nominations for club president, but she absolutely gave it a cross, and it became out better for her and for all people. Getting out of that comfort area gave her a brand new enjoy and know-how of herself. Now she is privy to that she is able to extra matters, resulting in a lift in her conceitedness.

Stepping out of doors of your consolation location doesn't mean which you throw your self in the face of hazard. It technique that you are trying new things and studying to face new types of disturbing situations.

Stop with all of the comparisons: We are all responsible of this.

"I want I had as a bargain money as him..."

"I choice I had that get dressed..."

"I preference I must excursion like..."

We are vulnerable to evaluate ourselves to others for organic reasons. According to organizational behavior professional Thomas Musweiler, the assessment is "one of the maximum essential strategies we construct an cognizance of who we are, what we're suitable at, and what we're no longer so appropriate at." (Cruze, 2023)

Most of the time, this brainwork occurs within the historic beyond in a fraction of a 2nd without our expertise. But, if we generally base how we pick out to stay at the success and failures of various people's lives, it is able to grow to be poisonous. We do this subconsciously, however it is vital we paintings on being aware of this so that we understand the manner to save you it even because it's occurring and unhelpful.

Understand the fact that everybody's existence is specific. Before you subconsciously compare your life to someone else's, make an effort to understand what it's far that you cost. If you don't measure achievement via the kind of vehicle you electricity, there's no reason to be jealous of someone else's new vehicle. The same can be actual for some thing; for any stuff they collect, testimonies they have got, or subjects that they do. The pleasant individual you need to assess yourself to is you.

What I advise with the beneficial aid of that is that I want to ask myself the query, "What would possibly my future self tell me to do nowadays". If my destiny self is happy with my nowadays self, then I experience top notch about how I have a look at. Notice it's the destiny self and now not the beyond self... there's no want to be crucial of your past. Instead, recognition on making friends along with your future self and having notable conversations with that character.

Let skip of the beyond: Holding straight away to the beyond and letting it cross can every be aware options, no matter the truth that we may not apprehend it. Everyone has had terrible and demanding critiques in their lives; a few people's memories are arguably worse than others, but we are all state of affairs to harm, ache, and loss in our lives. Like me, you've got had been given had your honest percentage of terrible opinions too.

Because of that, in some unspecified time in the destiny on your lifestyles, you've got puzzled the way to flow into on out of your painful beyond. Your gift emotional struggling is intently related to your past. While it is not possible with a purpose to delete the reminiscences (nor do you ever really need to), it's far feasible to actually be given what's finished is completed, what you could and can't manage, take responsibility, and cognizance on the schooling that your evaluations have given you.

We can pick out to remind ourselves that our past, correct or terrible, has shaped who we are nowadays. But, it does no longer dictate our destiny. If we recognition on "what must had been," we are capable of in no manner be capable of attention on "what is probably". Learning from the experience and that specialize in improvement are of the finest techniques to surpass your past. Remember the quote:

Chapter 8: Get Comfortable With Small Talk

From Awkward Silence to Effortless Conversation

Ah, small communicate. They point out on my own can conjure up pictures of pressured smiles, strained pauses, and the determined desire to break out into the nearest air vent. We've all been there, trapped inside the linguistic purgatory of "How's the climate?" and "So, any fun weekend plans?" But right here's the secret: small communicate isn't a social sentence, it is a superpower. It's the bridge from stranger to acquaintance, the stepping stone to friendship, and the name of the sport sauce that makes existence's connections stick.

Let's be sincere, no matter the reality that, studying this art isn't precisely intuitive. It's like trying to juggle flaming chainsaws while faucet-dancing on a tightrope blindfolded – outstanding, yes, but moreover terrifyingly smooth to lessen to rubble. But worry not, fellow social butterfly wannabes! This chapter is your personal roadmap to conquering the small communicate jungle, leaving awkward silences extinct and attractive communication blossoming in their wake.

Step One: Reframe the Game:

First topics first, ditch the negativity Stop deliberating small communicates as a chore, a hurdle, or a social responsibility. Instead, see it as an adventure – a risk to discover hidden treasures within the form of charming people and surprising connections. Think of it like a recreation, one in that you are the captivating explorer, navigating the social landscape and discovering new worlds with each witty declaration and insightful question.

Step Two: Equip Yourself with Conversation Starters:

Let's face it, staring blankly at someone at the same time as crickets chirp inside the ancient past isn't precisely prevailing. So, come armed with some verbal exchange starters to interrupt the ice. News headlines, interesting observations approximately the environment, or perhaps a playful remark approximately their outfit – a few element is going! Just maintain in thoughts, the secret's to be authentic, curious, and open to wherein the verbal exchange could possibly take you.

Step Three: Master the Art of the Open-Ended Question:

Forget the "positive-or-no" traps. Instead, unharness your internal interviewer and craft questions that invite elaboration and spark right hobby. Ask approximately their interests, their passions, their goals – some thing that gets them talking beyond one-phrase answers. This no longer only continues the communication flowing, but it moreover offers you a glimpse into their worldwide, making them sense heard and valued.

Step Four: Become an Active Listener:

Remember, small communicate is not a monologue, it is a dance. So, placed away your telephone, silence your internal monologue, and actually be aware of what the possibility character is saying. Lean in, make eye contact, and show them you're engaged. Ask observe-up questions, nod thoughtfully, and offer actual reactions – let them apprehend their phrases depend.

Step Five: Embrace the Pause:

Silence isn't the enemy, it is a natural part of the verbal exchange go with the float. Don't panic if a beat of quiet falls – allow it grasp inside the air, enjoy it even. Use it as a 2d to gather your thoughts, approach what's been stated, or really revel in the relationship you're constructing.

Step Six: The Graceful Exit:

All unique topics should come to an give up, and so ought to small communicate. But do no longer without a doubt disappear into the night time time time. Acknowledge the communique, precise your pride in assembly them, and leave them with a real smile and a warm farewell. Remember, the remaining have an effect on is truely as important because the primary.

Bonus Tip: Be Yourself (with a Dash of Sparkle):

Above all, do not try to be a person you're now not. Let your character shine through, whether or not or now not or no longer you are the witty comic, the insightful observer, or the passionate storyteller. People are inquisitive about authenticity, so non-public your quirks, encompass your humor, and allow your specific spark moderate up the verbal exchange.

Remember, small speak isn't always about perfection, it is about connection. It's about constructing bridges, sparking hobby, and commencing doors to the fascinating worldwide of human interplay. So, bypass forth, my friend, and conquer the small talk jungle! With a piece exercise, a dash of braveness, and a whole lot of actual hobby, you will be leaving awkward silences in the dust and weaving connections that final a life-time.

And don't forget, the adventure is sincerely as essential because the vacation spot. So, revel in the technique, embody the stumbles, and feature a great time each verbal exchange, large or small, as a victory within the grand hobby of connecting with others. Now circulate forth, you social butterfly, and spread your wings!

Read Body Language Like a Book:

Unlocking the Hidden Messages in Every Gesture

Have you ever felt like you're having a beautifully incredible verbal exchange, however a few issue sincerely feels... Off? You go away the encounter feeling pressured, uncertain if you in reality related or absolutely exchanged pleasantries. The fact is, the phrases we talk are truely the top of the iceberg. Beneath the ground lies a massive ocean of unstated communication, a language woven from diffused shifts in posture, fleeting expressions, and the silent symphony of our our our bodies. This language, my buddy, is known as body language, and studying it is the key to unlocking the genuine depths of human interplay.

Think of your self as a detective, interpreting the clues that dance at some stage in a person's face, linger of their posture, and flicker in their gaze. Every crossed arm, every tense twitch, every raised eyebrow tells a story, prepared to be unearthed. Learning to check this language is not approximately thoughts-reading; it is about expertise the silent conversations that take region alongside the spoken ones, enriching our perception and remodeling our connections from superficial to considerable.

The Five Pillars of Body Language:

1. The Eyes: Windows to the soul, in fact. Eyes maintain a wealth of statistics. Dilated pupils talk of excitement, at the same time as constricted ones may additionally sign pain. A regular gaze conveys self belief, on the same time as darting eyes can trace at anxiety or deception. Learn to take a look at the diffused shifts, the fleeting glints, and the manner eyes linger or avoid.

2. The Posture and Gestures: Our our our bodies are like living barometers, continuously adjusting to our emotional united states of america. A relaxed, open posture with uncrossed arms speaks of ease and openness, on the same time as a hunched, closed-off stance can signal defensiveness or discomfort. Pay hobby to

the way people fidget, how they use their hands, and the angle of their torso. Every movement tells a tale.

three. The Head and Neck: Head tilts communicate volumes. A slight tilt in the course of you suggests interest and attentiveness, even as a tilt away can advocate boredom or battle of words. Watch for head nods, that could constitute settlement or encouragement, and the subtle tightening of the neck muscle businesses, frequently a telltale signal of frustration or anger.

4. The Distance: Our private area is a sacred bubble, and the way near or some distance we stand from someone well-known our stage of consolation and intimacy. Close proximity indicates believe and engagement, on the same time as a miles wider hole can advocate formality or reservation. Be privy to approaches human beings regulate their function close to you,

and don't hesitate to take a step once more if you enjoy soreness.

five. The Micro-expressions: These fleeting, lightning-rapid facial expressions are like blips at the emotional radar. A flicker of disgust, a touch of surprise, a micro-smile that disappears in an immediate – the ones subtle shifts can display hidden emotions and real intentions. Train your eye to trap the ones fleeting moments, and you could free up a deeper know-how of what's definitely taking region underneath the ground.

From Awareness to Connection:

Reading frame language is not about judgment or manipulation. It's approximately empathy, understanding, and building stronger, greater real connections. By acknowledging the unspoken messages, we are able to tailor our method, reply with sensitivity, and create a area in which right communication can flourish.

Imagine this: you're having a communique with someone, and they may be telling you approximately a hard scenario. You have a look at their arms crossed, their gaze averted, and a moderate tremor in their voice. Instead of urgent on, you lightly renowned their pain, offer a supportive gesture, and alter your tone to be more calming and statistics. This small shift, knowledgeable with the resource of your awareness of their frame language, should make a international of difference.

Beyond the Basics:

Remember, body language is a complicated dialect, and context is the whole lot. A crossed arm won't continually advise defensiveness, but as an alternative a comfortable stance. A fidgety hand might not be tension, but truly a frightened dependancy. The secret's to take a look at, check, and float-reference with one of a kind cues earlier than drawing conclusions.

Embrace the Challenge:

Learning to examine frame language is a lifelong adventure, a journey of discovery that unfolds with each interaction. It takes workout, staying electricity, and a willingness to step outside our private consolation location. But believe me, the rewards are immeasurable. Imagine navigating conversations with newfound self belief, building deeper connections, and information people on a degree you never belief feasible. So, open your eyes, song your senses, and prepare to embark on a captivating adventure into the world of unspoken communique.

Chapter 9: Create an Open and Approachable Vibe

From Wallflower to Magnet

Step right right right into a crowded room, and what do you word? There are wallflowers clinging to the rims, faces buried in phones, exuding an air of "don't speak to me." Then there are the magnets, the moths to the social flame. They draw you in with a smile, a welcoming stance, an energy that whispers, "Come nearer, permit's be a part of." What's their thriller? It's no longer magic, it's miles magnetism. And the splendid statistics? You can discover ways to manufacture it too.

The Aura of Approachability:

It's now not just about appears, although self belief and a properly-groomed appearance really upload polish. It's approximately some component deeper, a vibe that radiates from within. It's the way you maintain your shoulders, the warmth to your eyes, the subtle tilt of your head that asserts, "I'm open, I'm fascinated, I'm happy to be proper right here."

Building Your Magnetic Field:

Here's your toolkit for crafting an approachable air of secrecy:

1. The Power of Posture: Stand tall, pals. Chin up, shoulders decrease back, not stiff or army-like, however comfortable and assured. Think of yourself as a lighthouse, beaming your presence out into the arena. Avoid slouching, crossed arms, and fidgeting – those are roadblocks to connection.

2. The Smile that Melts Icebergs: A right smile is a famous passport to approachability. It's not a plastered grin, but a warm temperature that reaches your eyes. Smile at strangers in the elevator, the barista, the character walking their canine. You'd be amazed how many smiles bounce back.

three. Eye Contact: The Bridge of Connection: Make eye touch, maintain it for a beat, and then allow it skip clearly. Don't stare, it's miles creepy. But don't dart around the room like a hummingbird on Red Bull. Eye contact says, "I see you, I'm gift, I'm inquisitive about what you have were given to say."

4. The Unfurling of Openness: Uncross your palms, uncrossed your legs. Let your frame be a welcoming region. Open arms, cushty arms, those are nonverbal invites. Avoid fidgeting at the side of your smartphone, your hair, your nails – the ones say, "I'm distracted, I'm not in reality right here."

five. Curiosity: The Magnet's Fuel: Be without a doubt curious approximately the human beings round you. Ask questions, pay interest actively, display interest of their lives. People gravitate towards folks who cause them to experience visible and heard.

6. The Language of Positivity: Ditch the negativity, the gossip, the complaints. Focus at the fine, the interesting, the things that spark satisfaction. Your strength is contagious, so choose to unfold the type that makes human beings want to be spherical you.

From Wallflower to Social Butterfly:

Remember, approachability isn't a switch you switch on; it's miles a muscle you teach. The more you exercise, the greater herbal it becomes. Start small, smile at a person on the bus, ask a proper query to the man or woman in line subsequent to you. You might be surprised at how your non-public self guarantee grows with every interaction.

The Ripple Effect of Magnetism:

And proper right right here's the lovely issue approximately approachability: it's miles contagious. When you radiate openness, it conjures up others to do the identical. You end up a catalyst for connection, a spark that ignites conversations and friendships inside the maximum surprising places. So, step out of your comfort quarter, encompass your inner magnet, and watch as the world round you opens up in strategies you by no means imagined.

Bonus Tip: Fake it until you're making it! Sometimes, all it takes is a little out of doors attempt to kickstart the internal shift. Stand a bit taller, stress a grin, ask a query – and shortly sufficient, the real warm temperature will have a look at.

Remember, you're a social superpower equipped to be unleashed. Go forth and magnetize the place!

Use Questions to Get to Know People Fast:

From Shallow Chats to Deep Connections

Have you ever sat through a communique that felt like chewing on cotton sweet: sweet, fluffy, but in the long run without substance? We've all been there, trapped in the purgatory of "How's the climate?" and "So, what do you do for artwork?" longing for some thing deeper, a few issue that in reality sparks a connection. But worry not, fellow explorers of the human coronary heart! This bankruptcy is your map to navigating the conversational jungle, armed with the most effective device of all: the art of asking questions.

Think of questions as tiny pickaxes, chipping away at the floor of small talk and revealing the hidden veins of gold inside. They're not interrogations, however invitations, mild nudges that bring about testimonies untold, passions unshared, and connections solid in the hearth of actual interest.

Ditch the Drill Sergeant Approach:

Forget the quick-fireplace Q&A. The aim is not to bombard someone with a barrage of inquiries, but to create a vicinity for open talk, wherein questions are stepping stones, not hurdles. Ask one question at a time, pay hobby attentively to the answer, after which, like a skilled cartographer, look at the path their terms display.

Befriend the Open-Ended Friend:

"Yes" or "no" answers are verbal exchange vain ends. Instead, encompass the open-ended question, your satisfactory community conversational compass. Ask such things as "What added you right right here these days?" or "What's a few thing you're obsessed with?" These are pathways predominant to winding trails of tales, ideals, and goals, geared up to be explored.

The Power of "Why" and "How":

These terms are your thriller guns. "Why" ignites the spark of introspection, inviting humans to percentage their motivations, their values, the fireside that burns inner them. "How" delves deeper, uncovering the information, the reviews that shaped their attitude, the brushstrokes that paint their precise story.

Go Beyond the Surface:

Don't settle for the number one layer. Ask follow-up questions, the curious whispers that say, "Tell me more." When someone mentions a interest, ask what they love about it. When they proportion a venture, inquire about the instructions discovered. These examine-united statesare like slight waves, washing away the floor and revealing the hidden depths.

Embrace the Unexpected:

Be organized for the instant the communication takes a detour. Let their answers be your guide, not your rigid script. Follow the sudden twists and turns, the digressions that result in hidden gem stones you in no way knew existed. The maximum giant connections frequently bloom in the fertile soil of serendipity.

Silence is Your Ally:

Don't fear the pause. Let the silence be a bridge, not a chasm. Give them space to ponder your questions, to gather their thoughts, to weave their personal narrative. Sometimes, the most profound answers are born inside the quiet space amongst phrases.

Remember, You're Not an Interrogator, You're an Explorer:

Your aim isn't to extract records, but to construct a bridge. Approach each communication with authentic interest, with a desire to recognize, now not judge. Listen along facet your coronary coronary heart, now not just your ears, and allow your self to be captivated via way of the memories that spread.

From Small Talk to Shared Souls:

Asking the proper questions isn't approximately gathering statistics; it is approximately developing connections. It's about peeling again the layers, uncovering the beauty and complexity that lies beneath the floor. With each question you ask, with each story you concentrate, you gather bridges of understanding, forge bonds of empathy, and create connections that closing a lifetime.

So, circulate forth, fellow questioner! Arm yourself with hobby, wield your questions with care, and embark on a adventure to find out the hidden treasures inside the human coronary heart. You would probably truly be amazed at the depths you discover, both in others and in yourself.

Bonus Tip: Don't be afraid to ask non-public questions! Of path, apprehend of context and luxury levels, however right inquiries approximately someone's passions, fears, or desires can reason the most huge connections.

Remember, questions are not definitely device for conversation; they are keys that free up the doors to the human soul. Open the ones doors with curiosity and kindness, and you can find out a international of marvel waiting to be explored.

Chapter 10: Find Common Ground

From Strangers to Soulmates (Well, Maybe Not That Fast, But You Get the Idea)

Have you ever sat in the course of from a person, a void stretching among you wider than the Grand Canyon, wondering the way to bridge the gap? Or perhaps you've got got met someone who appears captivating, however their lifestyles seems like a completely unique planet from yours? Fear now not, fellow social architects! This economic smash is your blueprint for constructing bridges of connection, one shared hobby at a time.

The Glue of Rapport: Finding Common Ground

Ever heard the pronouncing, "Birds of a feather flock together"? There's a reason for that. We're without a doubt inquisitlve about people who percent our pursuits, values, and memories. It's like locating a mystery language, a code most effective the ones within the understand can decipher. So, how do you faucet into this magic?

1. The Art of Active Listening:

Forget multitasking. Put away your telephone, silence your inner monologue, and supply the character your complete interest. Listen not really together together with your ears, but collectively with your coronary coronary heart. Pay attention to their terms, their body language, the subtle nuances that display their passions and priorities.

2. The Detective's Toolkit: Asking Insightful Questions:

Don't count on. Ask questions that probe past the floor. What are they passionate about? What makes them laugh? What's the most important project they have overcome? These questions are like shovels, digging for the hidden treasures of common ground.

3. The Unexpected Treasures of Shared Experiences:

We all have recollections. Funny ones, unhappy ones, ones that fashioned who we are. Look for techniques to attach your non-public reports to theirs. Did you each excursion to Thailand? Did you each have a canine named Sparky who chewed on the couch? These shared moments, no matter how small, are the bricks that build the bridge of rapport.

4. The Power of Vulnerability: Sharing Your Own Story:

People connect with human beings, now not facades. Don't be afraid to percentage your private memories, your passions, your vulnerabilities. This isn't always about bragging; it is about developing an invite, a vicinity wherein the opportunity character can sense snug reciprocating.

five. Celebrate the Differences:

Common floor is notable, however do not mistake it for a one-manner street. Embrace the variations, the perfect views, the stories that make you every who you are. These variations can upload spice, depth, and an entire lot of captivating communique to the aggregate.

From Strangers to Storytellers:

Building rapport isn't about finding clones of ourselves. It's approximately appreciating the tapestry of human experience, finding the threads that be part of us, and celebrating the stunning variations that weave the cloth of our lives.

Remember, rapport isn't a vacation spot, it's miles a journey. It's a dance of discovery, a shared exploration of the fascinating landscapes that lie internal every unique. So, take a step, ask a query, percentage a tale, and watch because the invisible bridge of connection stretches at some stage in the void, bringing you nearer, one heartbeat at a time.

Bonus Tip: Don't underestimate the strength of humor! A properly-timed shaggy dog tale, a playful statement, can damage down partitions and construct immediately rapport. Just bear in mind, preserve it mild and respectful.

So, move forth, connection architects! Build bridges together in conjunction with your phrases, pave paths in conjunction with your reminiscences, and watch as the arena opens as plenty as you in techniques you in no way imagined.

Master the Art of Reciprocity:

From Conversational Takers to Balanced Givers

Have you ever felt like you are caught within the one-sided tango of communique? You pour out tales, ask questions, and provide endless enthusiasm, whilst the alternative person sits again, a silent observer in your monologue. Or perhaps you have got got been at the receiving stop, bombarded with non-forestall chatter, leaving you tired and longing for a risk to breathe. Fear not, fellow conversational navigators! This financial disaster is your compass for locating the sweet spot, the elusive dance of reciprocity wherein conversations flow like a properly-choreographed waltz.

The Rule of Reciprocity: Give and Get in Equal Measure

Imagine a seesaw. On one thing, infinite talking, overflowing with anecdotes and evaluations. On the opportunity, a deafening silence, punctuated pleasant with the beneficial resource of the occasional grunt of acknowledgment. This, my friends, is the conversational seesaw lengthy gone wrong. The key to reading this artwork is balance, the sensitive dance of giving and receiving, of listening and talking in equal degree.

Step One: Embrace the Power of Listening

Conversations are not one-guy suggests. They're collaborations, duets in which every voice merits to be heard. Put away your cellular telephone, silence your internal monologue, and genuinely concentrate. Make eye touch, nod thoughtfully, and provide encouraging activates like "Tell me extra" or "That's captivating, why?" Let the opportunity man or woman understand they have got your complete hobby, that their phrases depend.

Step Two: The Art of the Thoughtful Response

Don't sincerely react, reply. Listen for the deeper which means, the unspoken feelings at the back of the words. A considerate response isn't always a regurgitation of records, it is a bridge, a connection that suggests you apprehend and apprehend what they've shared. Ask examine-up questions, offer your personal perspective without hijacking the communication, and motive them to experience heard and understood.

Step Three: Share, But Don't Monopolize

Sharing your non-public testimonies is vital for building rapport, but take into account, it is not a solo act. Don't permit your anecdotes turn out to be a tidal wave, drowning out the opportunity individual's voice. Gauge their hobby, keep your testimonies relevant, and go away room for them to percentage their very own studies. Remember, the conversation is a shared place, not a private soapbox.

www.ingramcontent.com/pod-product-compliance
Lightning Source LLC
Chambersburg PA
CBHW071445080526
44587CB00014B/2002